Centered o

MW00906444

About This Book 2

The Piggy Press 3
- ◯ Identifying simple synonyms and antonyms
- ◉ Identifying more complex synonyms and antonyms

Ant Champs 11
- ◯ Identifying word families: *-ack, ick*
- ◉ Identifying word families: *-oke, -ight*

Bunny's Bloomin' Blossoms 19
- ◯ Identifying short vowels
- ◉ Identifying short and long vowels

Words Rock! 27
- ◯ Identifying initial blends: *sn, tr*
- ◉ Identifying initial blends: *str, thr*

Hot-Diggity Dog Bones! 35
- ◯ Identifying beginning digraphs: *sh, ch*
- ◉ Identifying beginning and ending digraphs: *sh, ch*

Art Shop 43
- ◯ Sorting *r*-controlled vowels: *ar, ir, or*
- ◉ Sorting and identifying the spelling of *r*-controlled vowels: *ar, ir, or*

Let's Do Lunch! 51
- ◯ Identifying prefixes: *un-, re-*
- ◉ Identifying prefixes: *pre-, dis-*

Supersize Snacks 59
- ◯ Identifying suffixes: *-ful, -able*
- ◉ Identifying suffixes: *-less, -ness*

Cuckoo Clucks 67
- ◯ Identifying parts of speech: nouns
- ◉ Identifying parts of speech: nouns, verbs

Bookworm Buddies 75
- ◯ Identifying ending punctuation and capitalization: months, days of the week
- ◉ Identifying ending punctuation and capitalization: holidays, locations, addresses

Just Like Peas in a Pod 83
- ◯ Counting to 1,000 by 2s, 5s, and 10s
- ◉ Counting to 1,000 by 25s, 50s, and 100s

.... 91
- ◯ Identifying place value to hundreds
- ◉ Identifying place value to thousands

Off to the Zoo! 99
- ◯ Adding basic facts to 10
- ◉ Adding basic facts to 18

Wiggle Round the Garden 107
- ◯ Subtracting from 8, 9, and 10
- ◉ Subtracting from 11, 13, and 18

Keep On Tractoring! 115
- ◯ Adding two-digit numbers without regrouping
- ◉ Adding two-digit numbers with regrouping

Game Time! 123
- ◯ Subtracting two-digit numbers without regrouping
- ◉ Subtracting two-digit numbers with regrouping

The Honey Hunt 131
- ◯ Multiplying by 2 and 5
- ◉ Multiplying by 3 and 4

Money in the Bank 139
- ◯ Identifying the value of mixed coins to 75¢
- ◉ Identifying the value of mixed coins to $1.00

Mouse Time 147
- ◯ Telling time: hour, half hour
- ◉ Telling time: half hour, quarter hour

Treasure Island 155
- ◯ Measuring length to the nearest inch
- ◉ Measuring length to the nearest centimeter

Answer Keys 163

Center Management Checklist 167

Centered on Success
Grade 2

Reinforce essential skills while promoting independent learning with the kid-pleasing center activities in *Centered on Success* for Grade 2! We've designed 20 all-new center activities to help you reinforce language arts and math skills through appropriately challenging learning experiences. Each center is adapted to two different skill levels or tasks, so you can match each activity to individual students' needs. For convenience, the two levels are color coded—yellow and blue—for easy identification and management. Simply choose a specific level for each student to complete, or encourage each child through both levels (first yellow, then blue).

Each center contains all the basic materials you need, including full-color, tear-out pages for easy center setup and implementation. Also included for your convenience are a center management checklist and answer keys.

Each center includes the following:

- an easy-to-scan teaching page with a skill description for each instructional level, a list of provided materials, step-by-step directions for preparing and using the center, and one or more center options for enhancing or extending the activity
- a full-color center mat, suitable for laminating
- first-level activity cards (yellow)
- second-level activity cards (blue)
- one reproducible recording sheet

Setting up the centers:

1. Tear out the perforated pages: teaching page, recording sheet (on back of teaching page), center mat, leveled activity cards.
2. Make a master copy of the student recording sheet.
3. Laminate the center mat and activity cards for durability.
4. Cut apart each set of leveled activity cards (yellow and blue).
5. Store the cards in resealable plastic bags. Place all center pieces in a large string-tie envelope. Label and store as desired.

Managing the centers:

1. Make a copy of the center checklist on page 167. Program the sheet with students' names and the center titles.
2. Choose a center and decide which level each student will complete.
3. Using a yellow or blue highlighter, mark the appropriate cell on the center checklist to indicate the level each student will complete. Set the checklist aside.
4. Place the center materials at a single-student center area.
5. Upon each student's completion of the center, assess understanding and mark the center checklist for each child accordingly.

The Piggy Press

 Identifying simple synonyms and antonyms

 Identifying more complex synonyms and antonyms

Materials:
supply of the recording sheet on page 4
center mat on page 5
trash cans and word bank card on page 7
trash cans and word bank card on page 9
2 resealable plastic bags
paper clip
sharpened pencil

Preparing the centers:
1. Laminate the center mat, trash cans, and cards if desired.
2. Cut out the cards and cans, and put each set into a separate bag.
3. Place the bags, center mat, sharpened pencil, paper clip, and copies of the recording sheet at a center.

Using the centers:
1. A student removes the cards from the bag and places the trash cans and the word bank card on the center mat where indicated.
2. She uses the pencil and paper clip to make a spinner, as shown, and then spins the paper clip.
3. She copies the word from the first trash can onto page 4.
4. She circles *synonym* or *antonym,* depending on where the spinner stops.
5. She uses the word bank card to help her write the synonym or antonym for the word.
6. She sets the trash can aside and continues in this same manner with the remaining trash cans.

Center Option
On the back of her recording sheet, have each student write a synonym for each word on the recording sheet marked *antonym* and write an antonym for each word marked *synonym.*

Name _____

The Piggy Press

Color the circle to match the back of your word bank card. ◯

Copy the word from the trash can.
Circle *synonym* or *antonym,* depending on where the spinner stopped.
Use the word bank card to help you write a synonym or antonym for the word.
Continue in this same manner with the remaining trash cans.

Word		Answer
	synonym antonym	
	synonym antonym	
	synonym antonym	
	synonym antonym	
	synonym antonym	
	synonym antonym	
	synonym antonym	
	synonym antonym	
	synonym antonym	
	synonym antonym	
	synonym antonym	
	synonym antonym	

©The Education Center, Inc. • *Centered on Success* • TEC60821 • Key p. 163

4 **Note to the teacher:** Use with the directions on page 3.

The Piggy Press

antonym

synonym

synonym

antonym

The Piggy Press

Editor Pig Lee Wiggly

1. Place the trash cans and word bank card on the center mat.
2. Use the pencil and paper clip to create a spinner; then spin the paper clip.
3. Complete page 4.

Place word bank card here.

Place trash cans here.

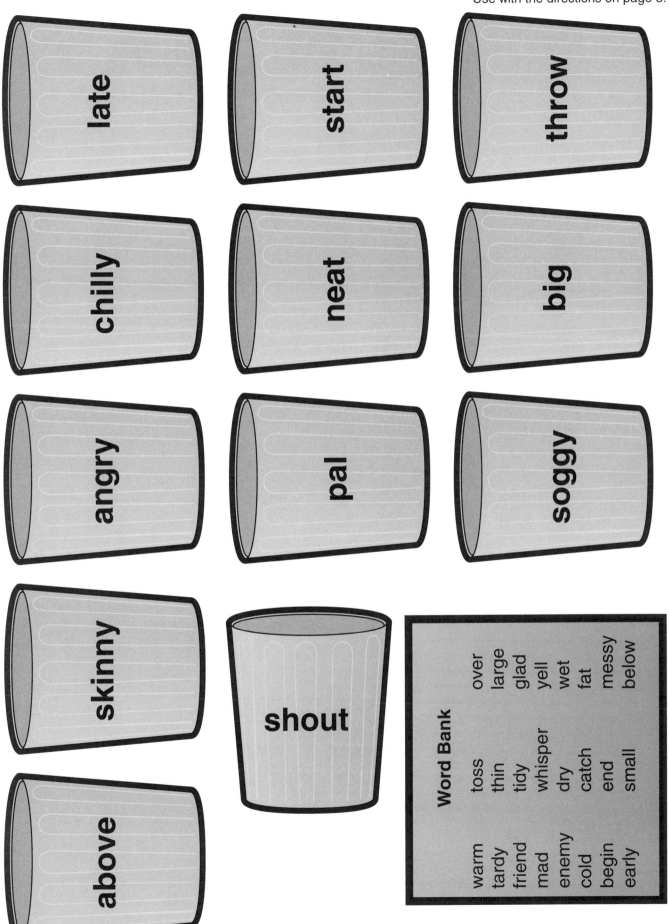

late

start

throw

chilly

neat

big

angry

pal

soggy

skinny

shout

above

Word Bank

warm	toss	over
tardy	thin	large
friend	tidy	glad
mad	whisper	yell
enemy	dry	wet
cold	catch	fat
begin	end	messy
early	small	below

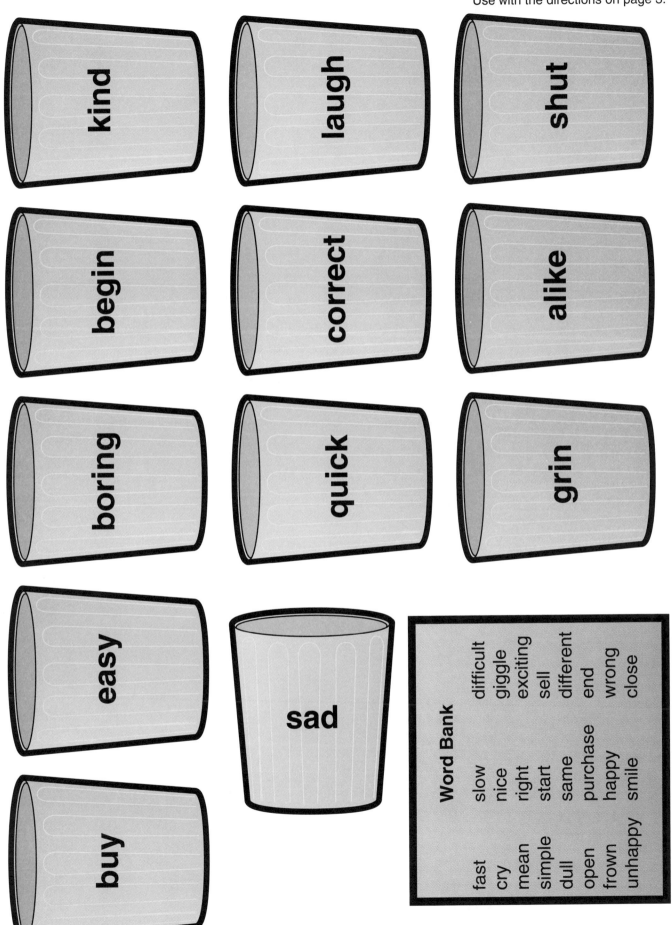

kind

laugh

shut

begin

correct

alike

boring

quick

grin

easy

sad

buy

Word Bank

fast   slow   difficult
cry   nice   giggle
mean   right   exciting
simple   start   sell
dull   same   different
open   purchase   end
frown   happy   wrong
unhappy   smile   close

Ant Champs

 Identifying word families: *-ack, -ick*

 Identifying word families: *-oke, -ight*

Materials:

supply of the recording sheet on page 12
center mat on page 13
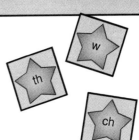 star and word family cards on page 15
star and word family cards on page 17
2 resealable plastic bags

Preparing the centers:

1. Laminate the center mat and cards if desired.
2. Cut out the cards and put each set into a separate bag.
3. Place the bags, center mat, and copies of the recording sheet at a center.

Using the centers:

1. A student removes the cards from the bag.
2. He places a word family card on each trophy where indicated.
3. He places each star card on the correct trophy to make a word.
4. He completes the recording sheet on page 12.

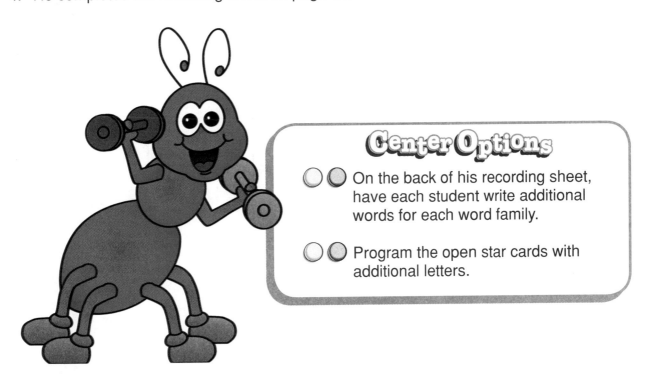

Center Options

○● On the back of his recording sheet, have each student write additional words for each word family.

○● Program the open star cards with additional letters.

Name _____

Ant Champs

Color the circle to match the backs of your star cards. ◯

Label each trophy to match your center mat.
Write each new word you made on the correct trophy.

©The Education Center, Inc. • *Centered on Success* • TEC60821 • Key p. 163

Note to the teacher: Use with the directions on page 11.

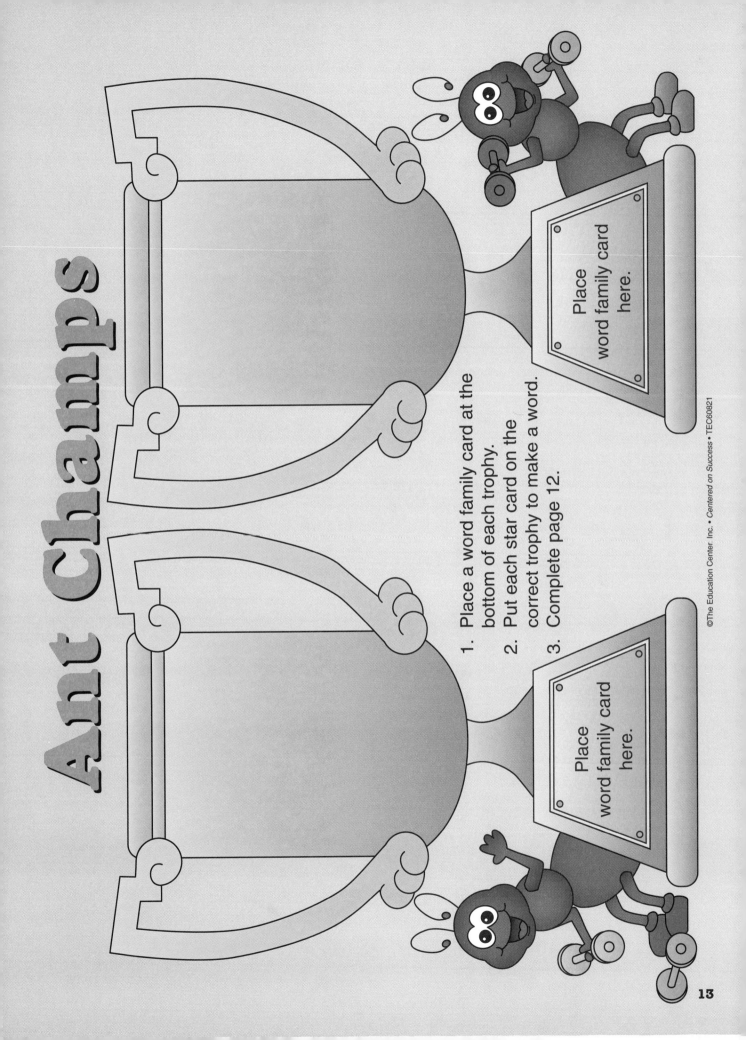

Ant Champs

1. Place a word family card at the bottom of each trophy.
2. Put each star card on the correct trophy to make a word.
3. Complete page 12.

Place word family card here.

Place word family card here.

-ack

-ick

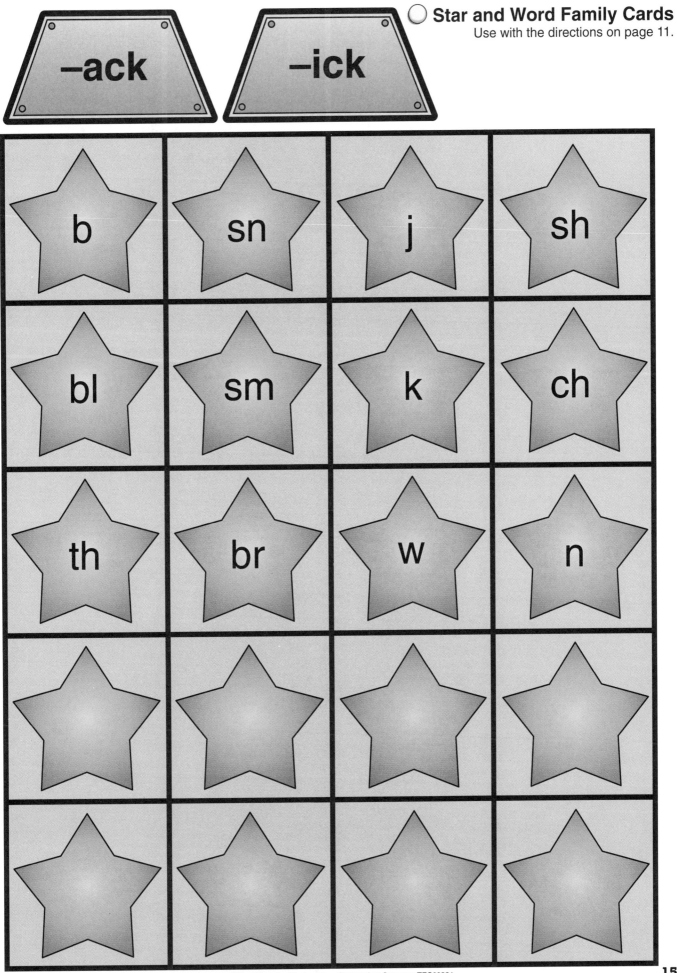

b

sn

j

sh

bl

sm

k

ch

th

br

w

n

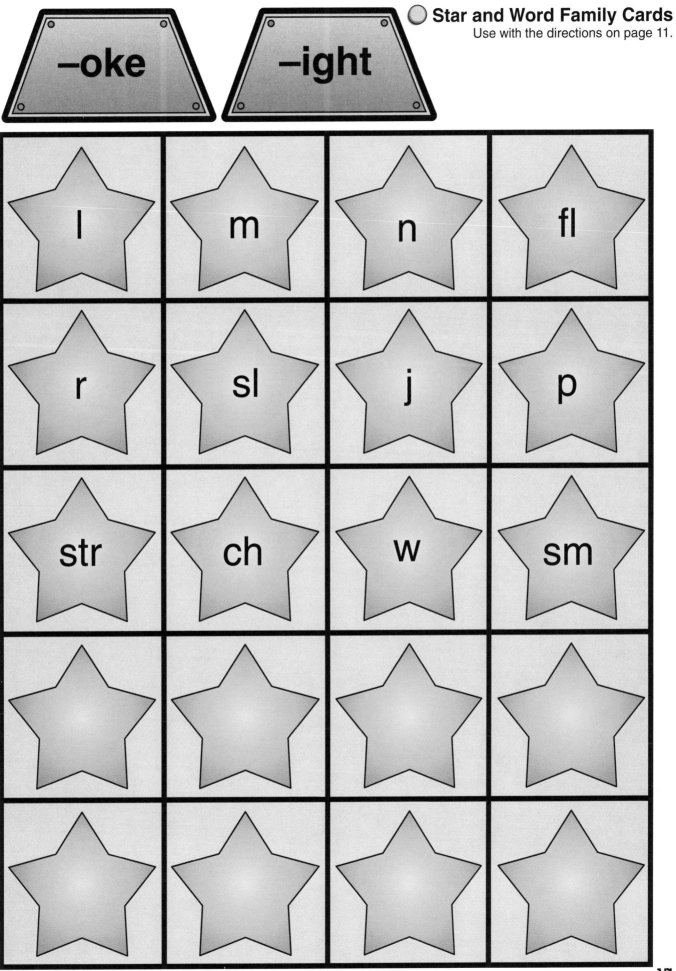

–oke

–ight

l	m	n	fl
r	sl	j	p
str	ch	w	sm

Bunny's Bloomin' Blossoms

 Identifying short vowels

 Identifying short and long vowels

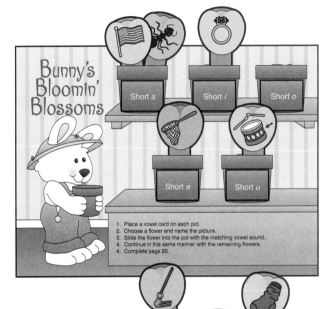

Materials:
supply of the recording sheet on page 20
center mat on page 21
flowers and vowel cards on page 23
flowers and vowel cards on page 25
2 resealable plastic bags

Preparing the centers:
1. Laminate the center mat, flowers, and vowel cards.
2. Cut out the flowers and cards and put each set into a separate bag.
3. Cut slits in the center mat where indicated.
4. Place the bags, center mat, and copies of the recording sheet at a center.

Using the centers:
1. A student removes the flowers and cards from the bag.
2. She places a card on each pot.
3. She names the picture on each flower and slides it in the pot with the matching vowel sound.
4. She completes page 20.

Center Option
On the back of her recording sheet, have each student write additional words for each vowel.

Bunny's Bloomin' Blossoms

Color the circle to match the backs of your center flowers. ◯

Label the pots to match your center mat.

Write the name of each picture on a flower in the correct pot.

Note to the teacher: Use with the directions on page 19.

Bunny's Bloomin' Blossoms

1. Place a vowel card on each pot.
2. Choose a flower and name the picture.
3. Slide the flower into the pot with the matching vowel sound.
4. Continue in this same manner with the remaining flowers.
4. Complete page 20.

21

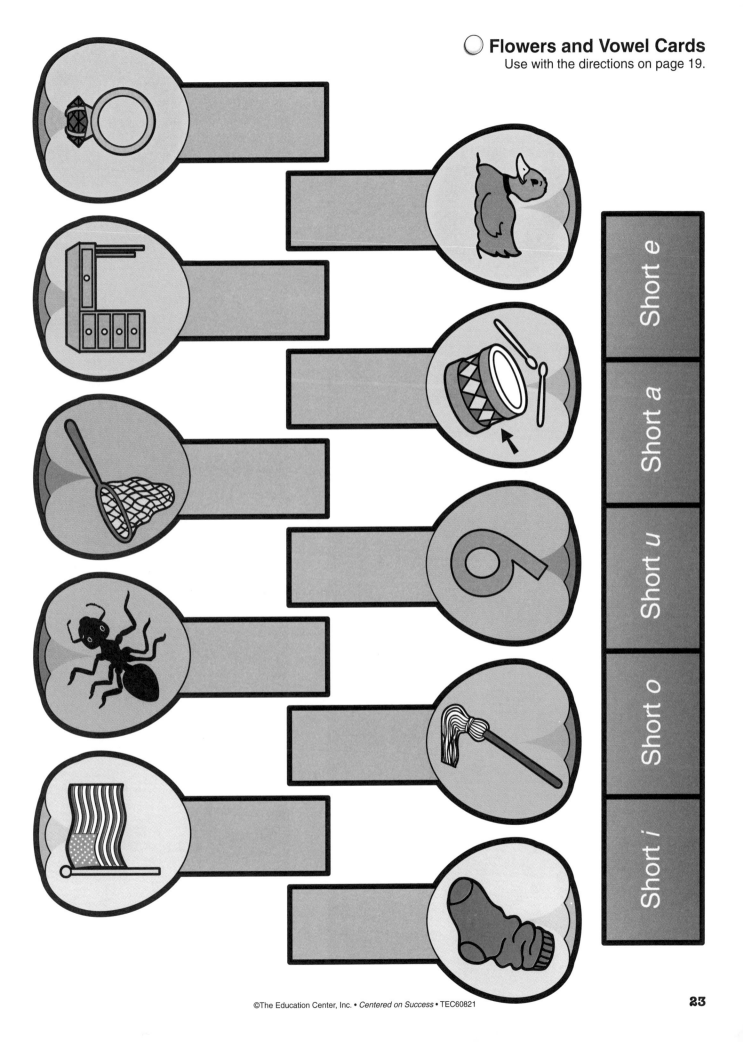

Short e

Short a

Short u

Short o

Short i

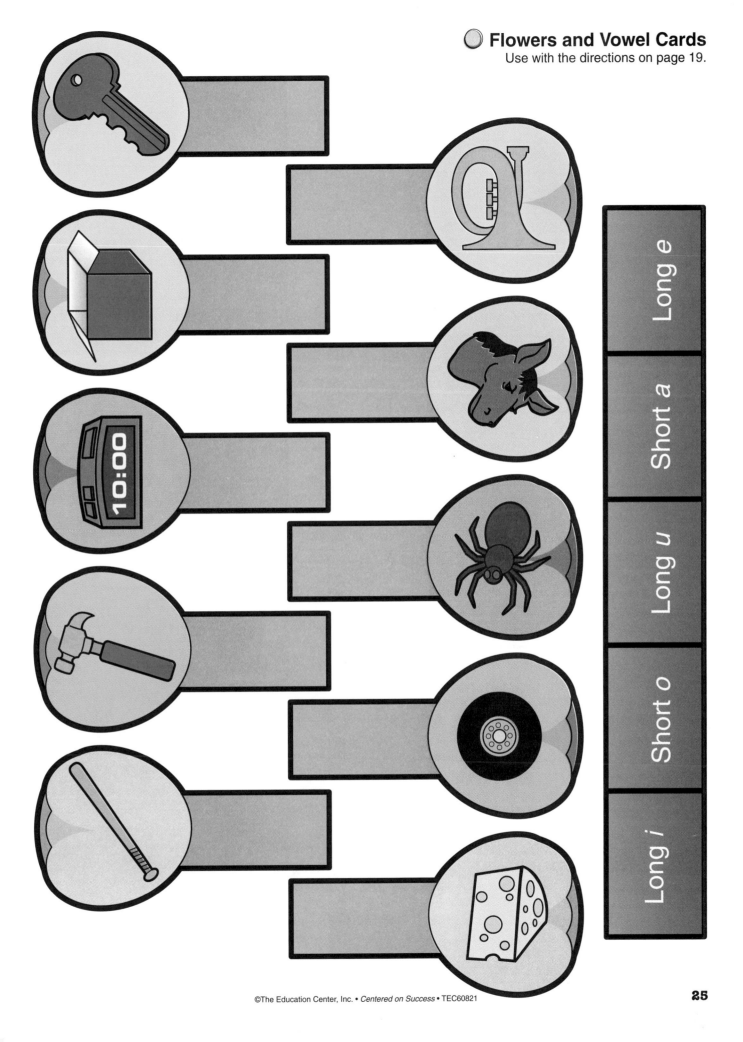

Long e

Short a

Long u

Short o

Long i

Words Rock!

Identifying initial blends: *sn, tr*

Identifying initial blends: *str, thr*

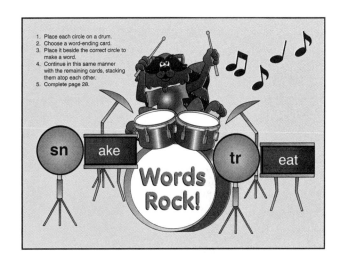

Materials:
supply of the recording sheet on page 28
center mat on page 29
circles and word-ending cards on page 31
circles and word-ending cards on page 33
2 resealable plastic bags

Preparing the centers:
1. Laminate the center mat, circles, and cards if desired.
2. Cut apart the circles and cards and put each set in a separate bag.
3. Place the bags, center mat, and copies of the recording sheet at a center.

Using the centers:
1. A student removes the circles and cards from the bag.
2. He lays the circles (blends) on the center mat.
3. He builds a word by selecting a word-ending card and placing it beside the correct blend.
4. He continues in this same manner with the remaining cards, stacking them atop each other.
5. He completes the recording sheet on page 28.

Center Option

On the back of his recording sheet, have the student write a sentence for one word from each list.

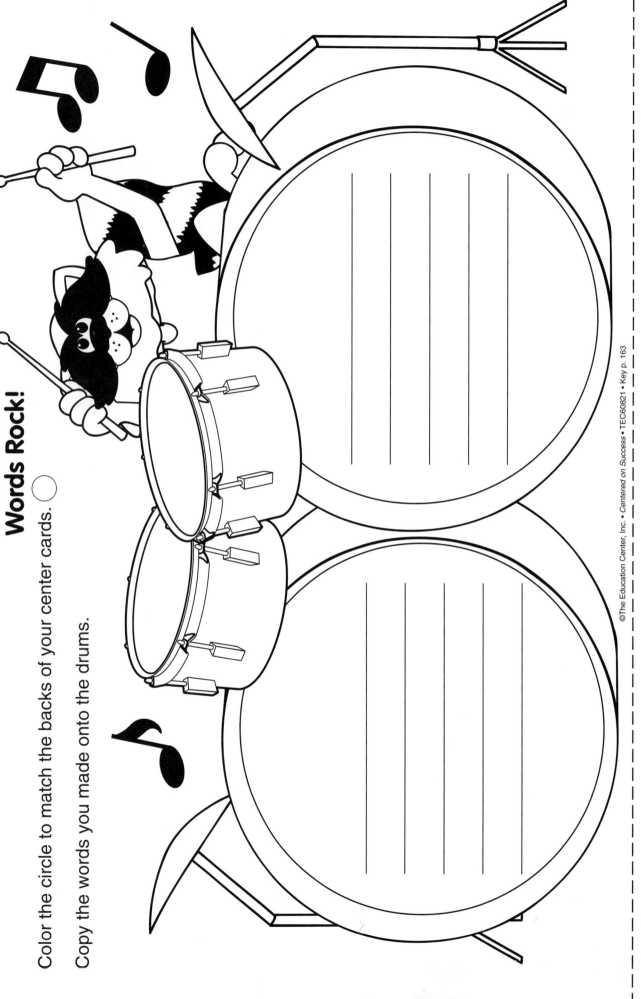

Name _____

28

Words Rock!

Color the circle to match the backs of your center cards. ◯

Copy the words you made onto the drums.

Note to the teacher: Use with the directions on page 27.

1. Place each circle where shown.
2. Choose a word-ending card.
3. Place it beside the correct circle to make a word.
4. Continue in this same manner with the remaining cards, stacking them atop each other.
5. Complete page 28.

Words Rock!

Place circle here.

Place circle here.

Place circle here.

eam	ead
eet	ill
ing	oat
and	eat
aw	ow

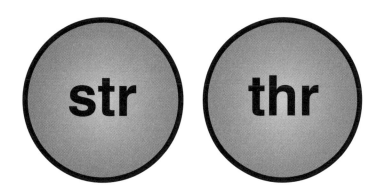

Hot-Diggity Dog Bones!

 Identifying beginning digraphs: *sh, ch*

 Identifying beginning and ending digraphs: *sh, ch*

Materials:
supply of the recording sheet on page 36
center mat on page 37
dog bones on page 39
dog bones on page 41
2 resealable plastic bags

Preparing the centers:
1. Laminate the center mat and dog bones if desired.
2. Cut out the bones and put each set into a separate bag.
3. Place the bags, center mat, and copies of the recording sheet at a center.

Using the centers:
1. A student removes the bones from the bag.
2. She places each whole bone, in turn, in the dirt on the center mat.
3. She lays a half bone atop each bone to make a word.
4. She completes the recording sheet on page 36.

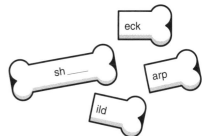

Center Options
On the back of her recording sheet, have each student write additional words for each digraph.

Store the bones in a clean, empty dog bone box.

Hot-Diggity Dog Bones!

Color the circle to match the backs of your center bones. ◯

Write each word you made on a bone.

Hot-Diggity Dog Bones!

FIDO

1. Place each dog bone, in turn, in the dirt.
2. Lay a half bone atop each bone to make a word.
3. Complete page 35.

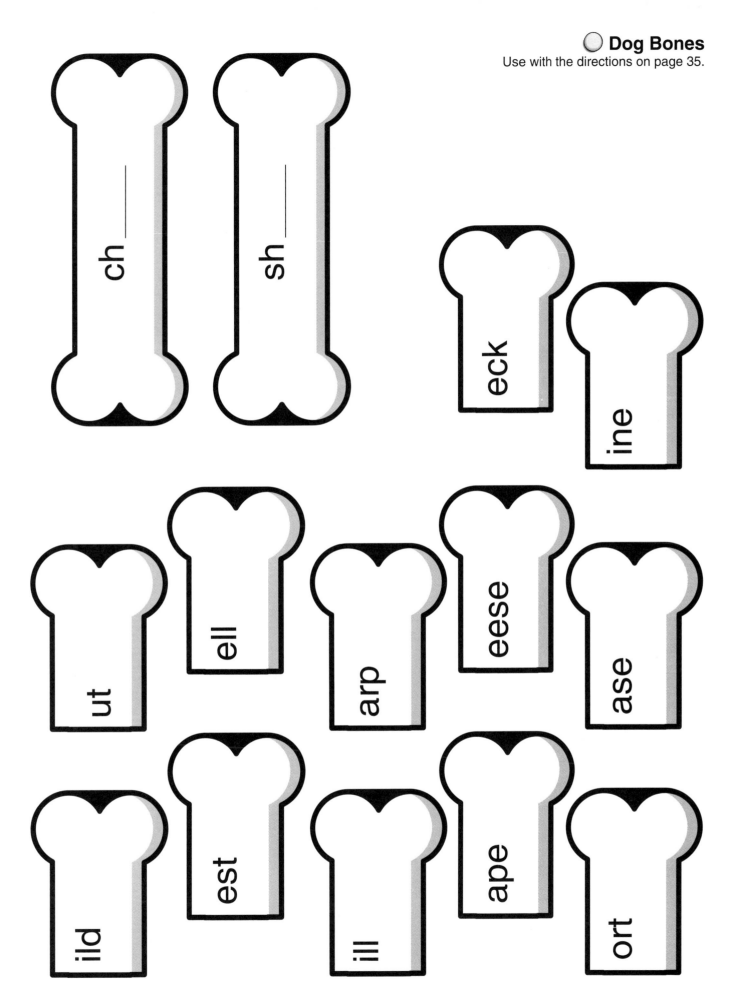

ch _____

sh _____

eck

ine

ut

ell

arp

eese

ase

ild

est

ill

ape

ort

Use with the directions on page 35.

ch___

sh___

___ch

___sh

icken

ri

alk

su

omp

mun

ark

da

irt

fi

are

bru

Art Shop

 Sorting *r*-controlled vowels: *ar, ir, or*

 Sorting and identifying the spelling of *r*-controlled vowels: *ar, ir, or*

Materials:
supply of the recording sheet on page 44
center mat on page 45
picture cards on page 47
picture cards on page 49
2 resealable plastic bags

Preparing the centers:
1. Laminate the center mat and picture cards if desired.
2. Cut apart the cards and put each set in a separate bag.
3. Place the bags, center mat, and copies of the recording sheet at a center.

Using the centers:
1. A student removes the cards from the bag and places them faceup in the center area.
2. He chooses a card and names the picture.
3. On the center mat, he finds the picture that has the same vowel pattern. He places the card in the box beside the picture.
4. He continues in this same manner with the remaining cards.
5. He completes the recording sheet on page 44.

Center Option
Invite the student to draw on the back of his recording sheet a different picture for each highlighted vowel sound and then label each picture.

Art Shop

Color the circle to match the backs of your center cards. ◯

Write the word for each picture below its matching vowel pattern.

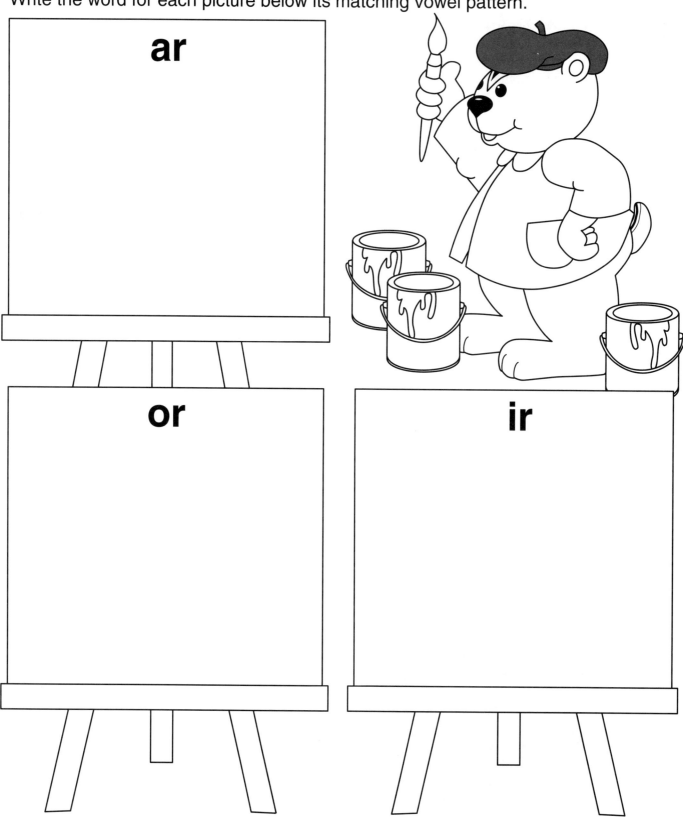

ar

or

ir

Art Shop

1. Place each card beside the picture with the matching vowel pattern.
2. Complete page 44.

car

corn

bird

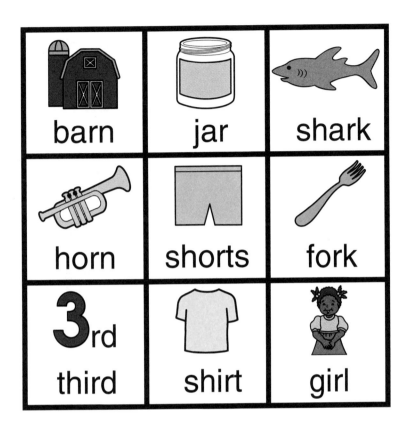

barn	jar	shark
horn	shorts	fork
third	shirt	girl

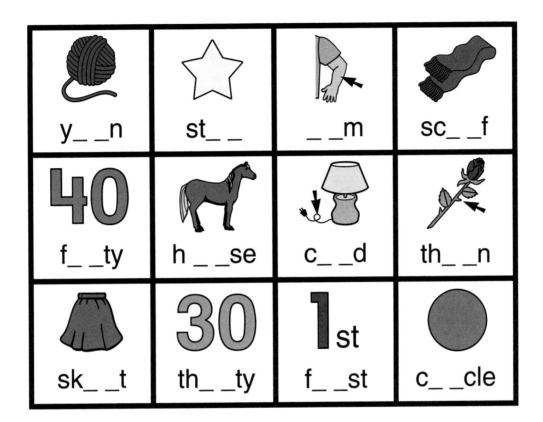

y_ _n | st_ _ | _ _m | sc_ _f

f_ _ty | h_ _se | c_ _d | th_ _n

sk_ _t | th_ _ty | f_ _st | c_ _cle

Let's Do Lunch!

 Identifying prefixes: *un-, re-*

 Identifying prefixes: *pre-, dis-*

Materials:
supply of the recording sheet on page 52
center mat on page 53
○ plates and sandwich cards on page 55
◉ plates and sandwich cards on page 57
2 resealable plastic bags

Preparing the centers:
1. Laminate the center mat, plates, and sandwich cards if desired.
2. Cut out the plates and sandwich cards and put each set into a separate bag.
3. Place the bags, center mat, and copies of the recording sheet at a center.

Using the centers:
1. A student removes the plates and sandwich cards from the bag.
2. She places the plates atop the plates on the center mat.
3. She reads the word on each sandwich card and places it on the correct plate to make a word.
4. She completes the recording sheet on page 52.

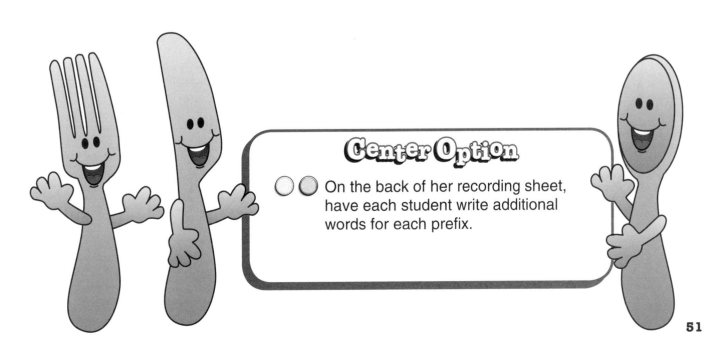

Center Option
○○ On the back of her recording sheet, have each student write additional words for each prefix.

Let's Do Lunch!

Color the circle to match the backs of your center plates. ◯

Label the napkins to match your center plates.
Write the new words you made with each prefix on the sandwich.

Let's Do Lunch!

1. Place a plate atop each plate on the center mat.
2. Read the word on each sandwich.
3. Place it on the correct plate to make a word.
4. Complete page 52.

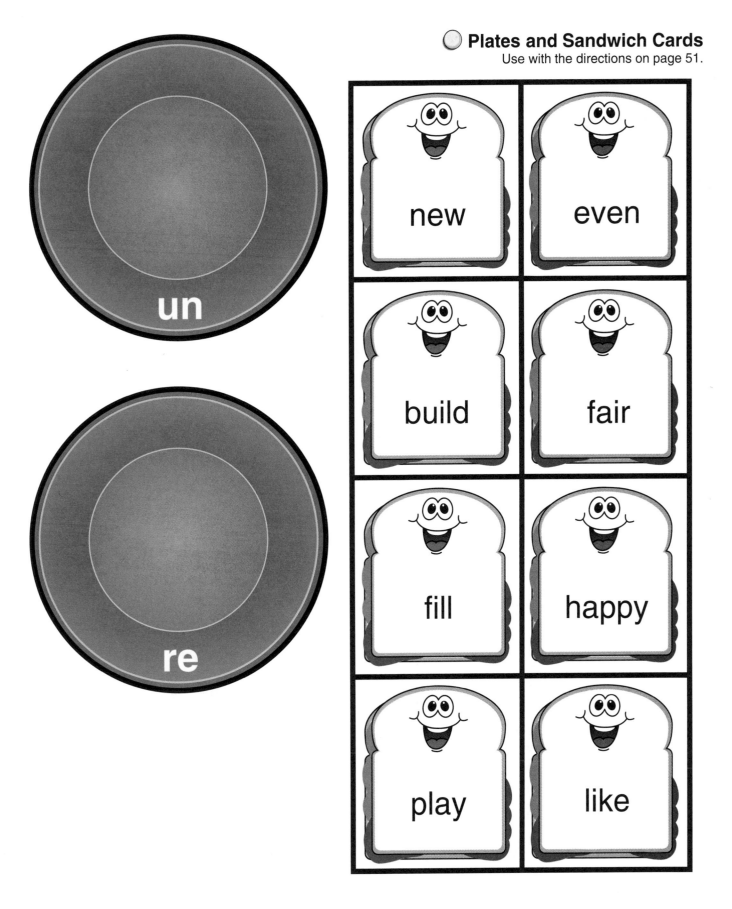

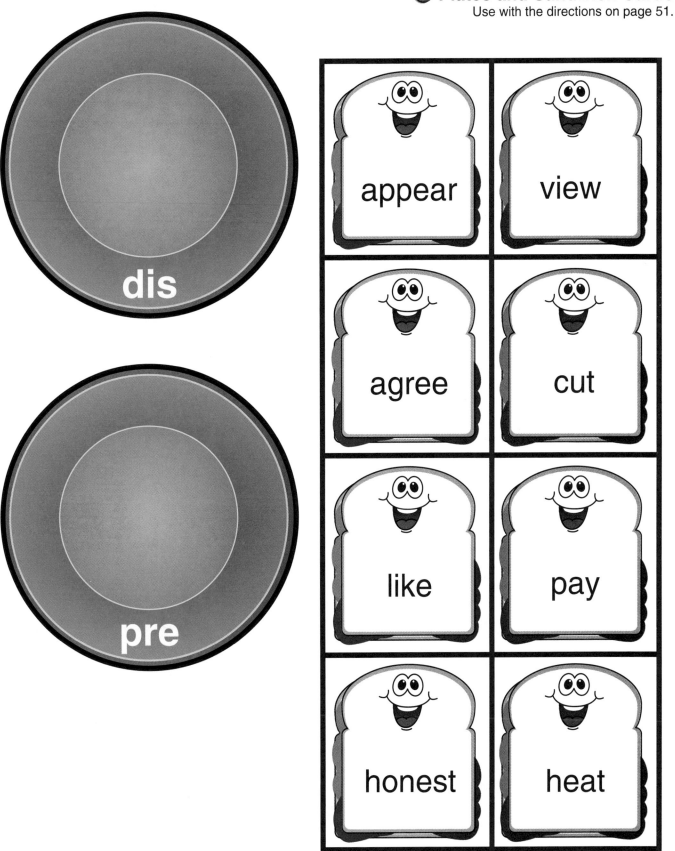

dis

pre

appear

view

agree

cut

like

pay

honest

heat

Supersize Snacks

 Identifying suffixes: *-ful, -able*

 Identifying suffixes: *-less, -ness*

Materials:
supply of the recording sheet on page 60
center mat on page 61
base word wheels and suffix cards on page 63
base word wheels and suffix cards on page 65
2 resealable plastic bags
2 paper clips
brad

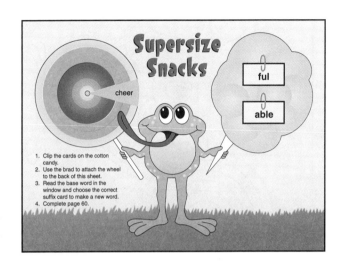

Preparing the centers:
1. Laminate the center mat, wheels, and cards.
2. Cut out the wheels and cards and put each programmed set into a separate bag.
3. Cut slits along the dotted lines on the center mat and insert paper clips.
4. Cut out the window in the center mat where indicated.
5. Poke a small hole through the black dot on each wheel and on the center mat.
6. Place the bags, brad, center mat, and copies of the recording sheet at a center.

Using the centers:
1. A student removes the wheels and cards from the bag.
2. He clips the suffix cards on the center mat where indicated.
3. He uses the brad to attach the wheel to the back of the center mat.
4. He reads the base word in the window and chooses the correct suffix to make a new word.
5. He copies the word he made on the recording sheet on page 60.
6. He continues in this same manner with the remaining base words.

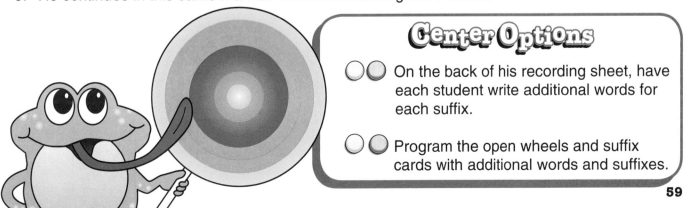

Center Options

On the back of his recording sheet, have each student write additional words for each suffix.

Program the open wheels and suffix cards with additional words and suffixes.

Name _____

60

Supersize Snacks

Color the circle to match the back of your center wheel. ⃝

Write the word you made below.
Continue in this same manner with the remaining base words.

_____

_____

_____

_____

_____

©The Education Center, Inc. • *Centered on Success* • TEC60821 • Key p. 164

Note to the teacher: Use with the directions on page 59.

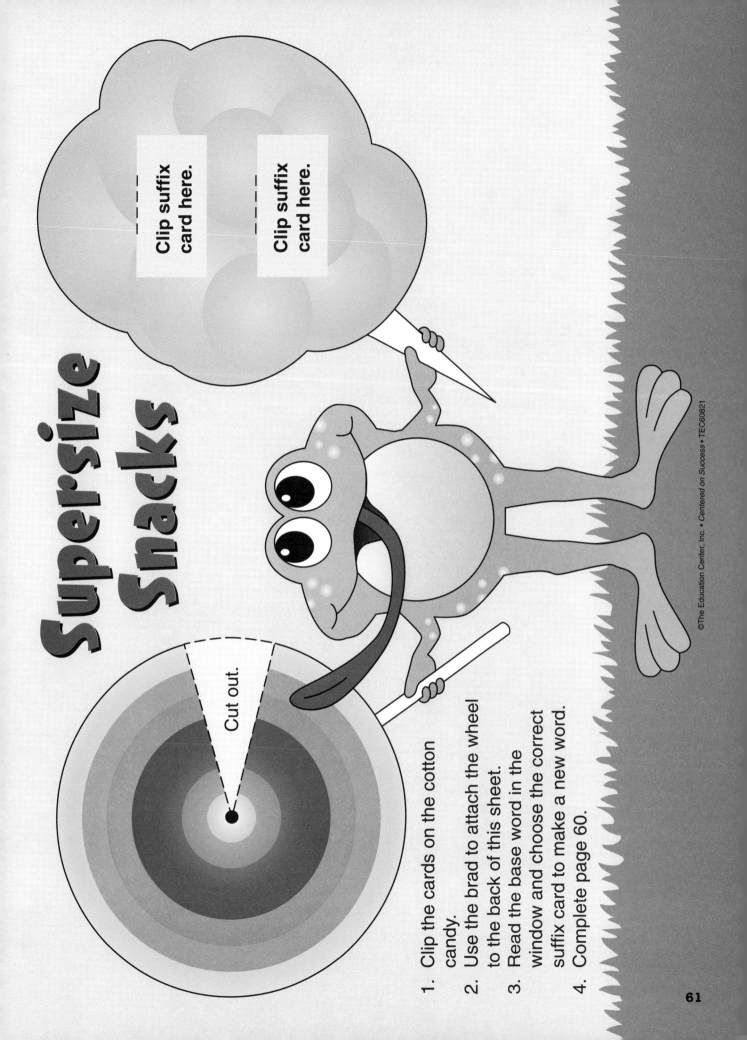

Supersize Snacks

Clip suffix card here.

Clip suffix card here.

Cut out.

1. Clip the cards on the cotton candy.
2. Use the brad to attach the wheel to the back of this sheet.
3. Read the base word in the window and choose the correct suffix card to make a new word.
4. Complete page 60.

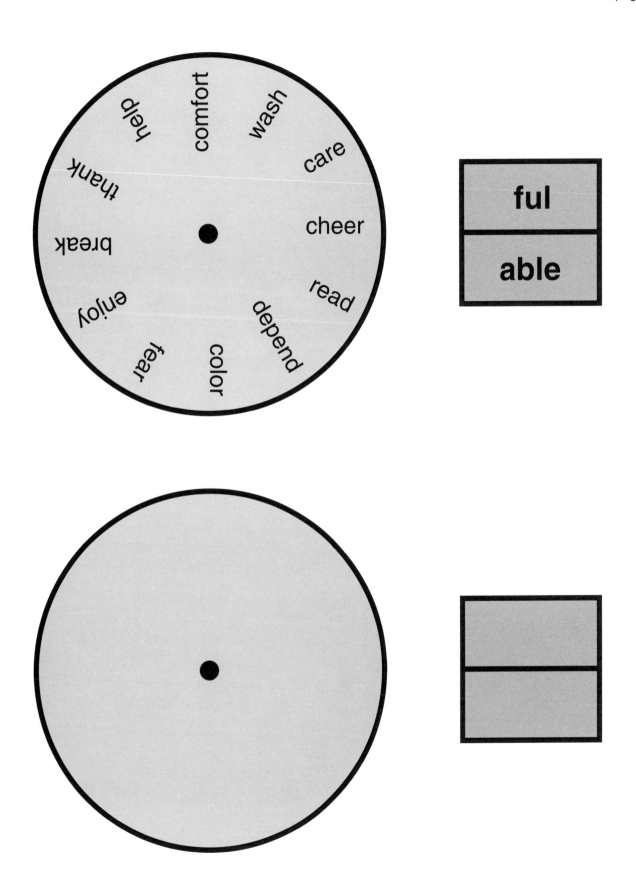

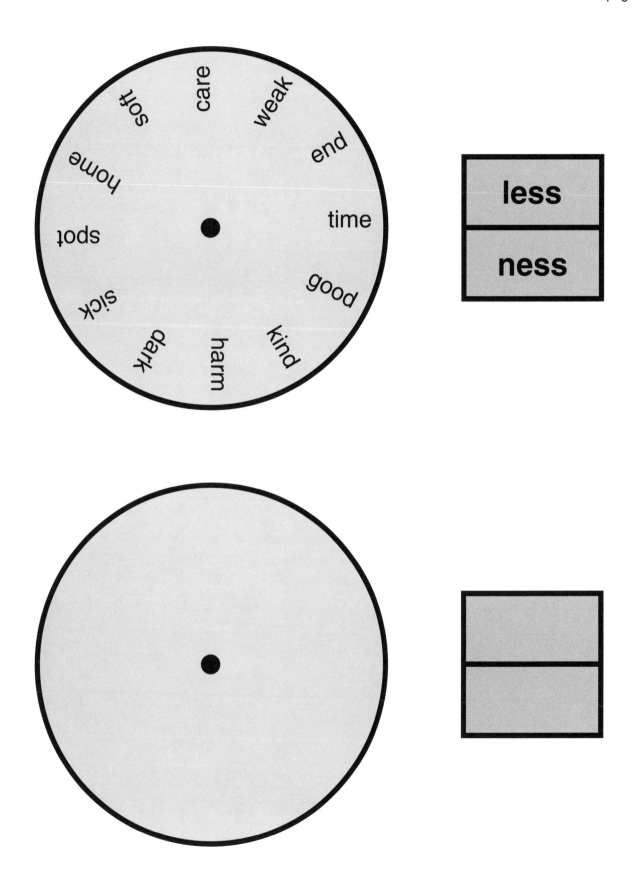

Cuckoo Clucks

 Identifying parts of speech: nouns

 Identifying parts of speech: nouns, verbs

Materials:
a supply of the recording sheet on page 68
center mat on page 69
eggs and label on page 71
eggs and label on page 73
2 resealable plastic bags

Preparing the centers:
1. Laminate the center mat, eggs, and labels if desired.
2. Cut out the eggs and labels. Put each programmed set into a separate bag.
3. Place the bags, center mat, and copies of the recording sheet at a center.

Using the centers:
1. A student removes the eggs and the label from the bag.
2. She places the label on the center mat where indicated.
3. She reads the word on each egg and places it on the correct nest.
4. She counts the eggs in the Nouns nest to determine whether there are six. If not, she reviews her choices and makes the appropriate changes.
5. She completes the recording sheet on page 68.

Center Options

⚪⚪ Program the open eggs with additional words.

⚪⚪ On the back of her recording sheet, have each student write additional words for each nest.

67

Cuckoo Clucks

Color the circle to match the backs of your center eggs. ◯

Label the nest at the right to match your center mat.
Copy each word on an egg in the correct nest.

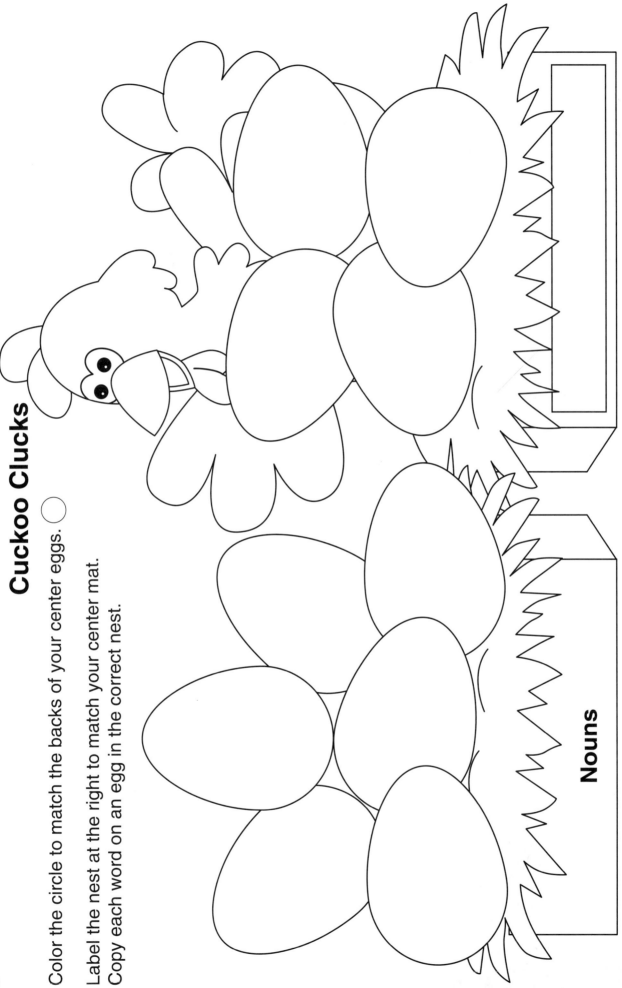

Nouns

Note to the teacher: Use with the directions on page 67.

Cuckoo Clucks

1. Place the label on the nest at the right.
2. Place each egg on the correct nest.
3. Count the eggs in the Nouns nest. Do you have 6?
4. If not, check your work.
5. Complete page 68.

Place label here.

Look! No hands!

Nouns

hay

egg

chicken

next

hat

other

the

beak

legs

silly

Not Nouns

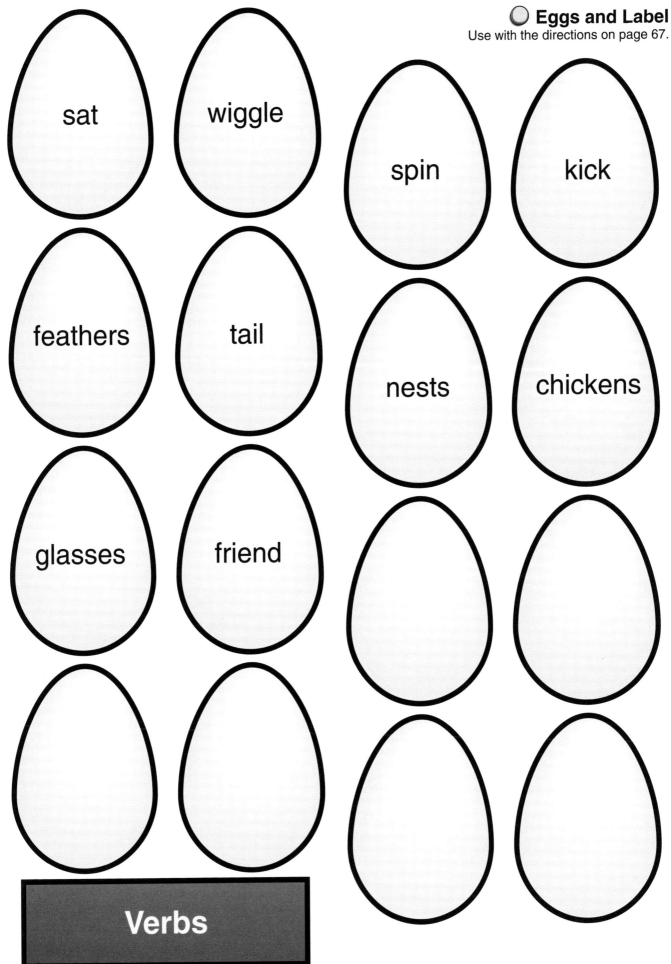

sat

wiggle

spin

kick

feathers

tail

nests

chickens

glasses

friend

Verbs

74

Bookworm Buddies

 Identifying ending punctuation and capitalization: months, days of the week

 Identifying ending punctuation and capitalization: holidays, locations, addresses

Materials:
supply of the recording sheet on page 76
center mat on page 77
○ books on page 79
◎ books on page 81
2 resealable plastic bags

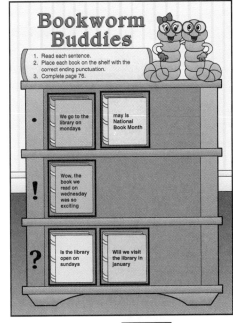

Preparing the centers:
1. Laminate the center mat and books if desired.
2. Cut out the books. Put each programmed set into a separate bag.
3. Place the bags, center mat, and copies of the recording sheet at a center.

Using the centers:
1. A student removes the books from the bag.
2. He reads the sentence on each book and places it on the shelf with the correct ending punctuation.
3. He copies each sentence onto the corresponding section of the recording sheet on page 76, correcting the capitalization error and adding the correct punctuation.

Center Options

○◎ On the back of his recording sheet, have each student write a sentence containing capitalization and punctuation errors. Have him challenge a classmate to correct it.

○◎ Program the open books with additional sentences that contain punctuation and capitalization errors.

Bookworm Buddies

Color the circle to match the backs of your center books. ◯

Write each sentence beside its correct ending punctuation.
As you write each sentence, fix the capitalization and ending punctuation mistakes.

_____

_____

_____

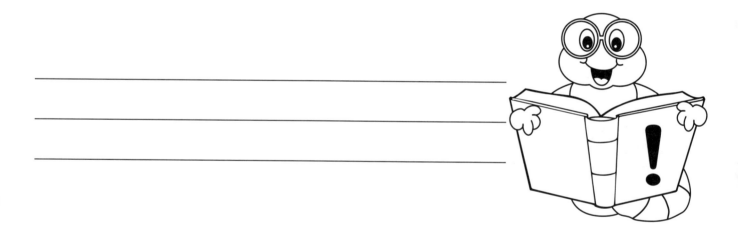

_____

_____

_____

_____

_____

_____

Bookworm Buddies

1. Read each sentence.
2. Place each book on the shelf with the correct ending punctuation.
3. Complete page 76.

.

!

?

We go to the library on mondays

may is National Book Month

An author is visiting in november

Wow, the book we read on wednesday was so exciting

Oh, my book was due on friday

Gee, I can't believe it's june already

Is the library open on sundays

Will we visit the library in january

Is this book due on tuesday

We are reading books about thanksgiving

The library is on main Street

there is a new computer in the library

Wow, halloween is in three days

Gosh, california is a big state

gee, this is the best book I've ever read

Will you read me a christmas story

Have you ever read about africa

Can you take me to Oak avenue

Just Like Peas in a Pod

 Counting to 1,000 by 2s, 5s, and 10s

 Counting to 1,000 by 25s, 50s, and 100s

Materials:
supply of the recording sheet on page 84
center mat on page 85
○ sets of peas and rule cards on page 87
◔ sets of peas and rule cards on page 89
2 resealable plastic bags

Preparing the centers:
1. Laminate the center mat and cards if desired.
2. Cut out the cards and put each set into a separate bag.
3. Place the bags, center mat, and copies of the recording sheet at a center.

Using the centers:
1. A student removes the cards from the bag.
2. She places a set of peas atop each pea pod on the center mat.
3. She matches the correct rule card to each set of peas.
4. She completes the recording sheet on page 84.

Center Option
○ ○ On the back of her recording sheet, have each student create an incomplete pattern. Have her challenge a classmate to complete it.

Just Like Peas in a Pod

Color the circle to match the backs of your center cards. ◯

Copy the numbers from each set of peas.
Write the missing numbers.
Write the rule.

_____, _____, _____, _____, _____, _____, _____, _____

Count by _____

_____, _____, _____, _____, _____, _____, _____, _____

Count by _____

_____, _____, _____, _____, _____, _____, _____, _____

Count by _____

_____, _____, _____, _____, _____, _____, _____, _____

Count by _____

_____, _____, _____, _____, _____, _____, _____, _____

Count by _____

_____, _____, _____, _____, _____, _____, _____, _____

Count by _____

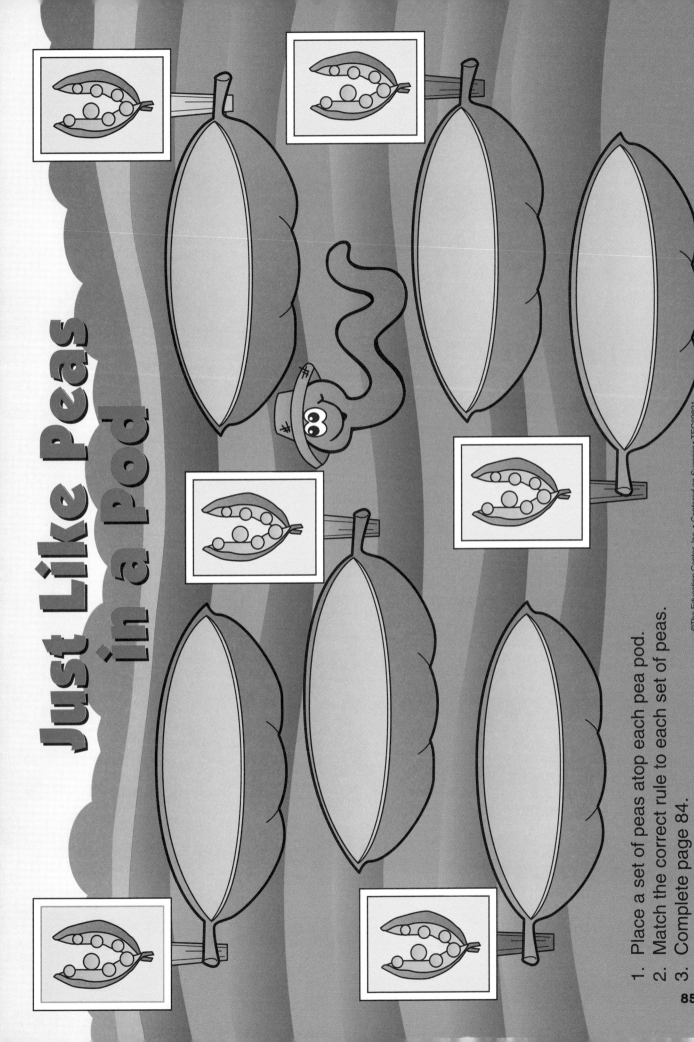

Just Like Peas in a Pod

1. Place a set of peas atop each pea pod.
2. Match the correct rule to each set of peas.
3. Complete page 84.

85

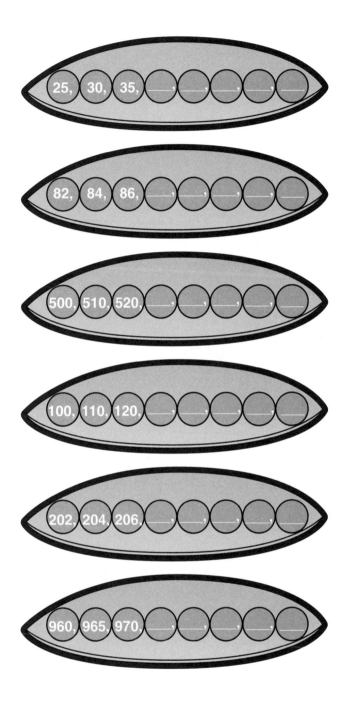

25, 30, 35, ___, ___, ___, ___, ___

82, 84, 86, ___, ___, ___, ___, ___

500, 510, 520, ___, ___, ___, ___, ___

100, 110, 120, ___, ___, ___, ___, ___

202, 204, 206, ___, ___, ___, ___, ___

960, 965, 970, ___, ___, ___, ___, ___

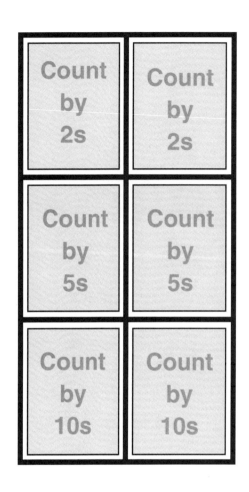

Count by 2s	Count by 2s
Count by 5s	Count by 5s
Count by 10s	Count by 10s

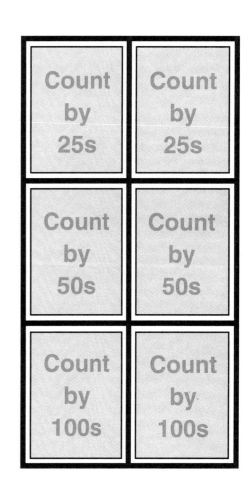

Sets of Peas and Rule Cards

Use with the directions on page 83.

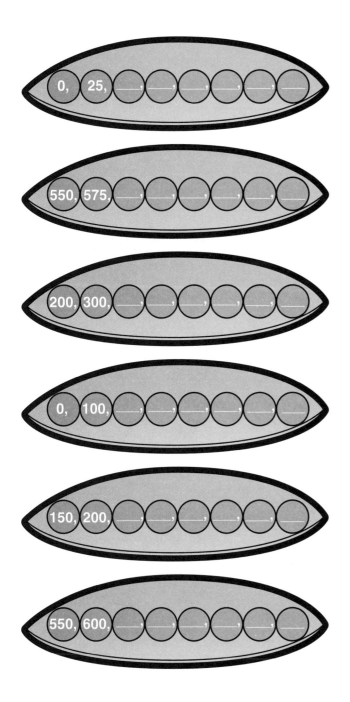

Count by 25s	Count by 25s
Count by 50s	Count by 50s
Count by 100s	Count by 100s

Gumballs Galore

 Identifying place value to hundreds

 Identifying place value to thousands

Materials:
supply of the recording sheet on page 92
center mat on page 93
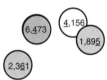 gumballs and labels on page 95
gumballs and labels on page 97
2 resealable plastic bags

Preparing the centers:
1. Laminate the center mat, gumballs, and labels if desired.
2. Cut out the labels and gumballs and put each programmed set in a separate bag.
3. Place the bags, center mat, and copies of the recording sheet at a center.

Using the centers:
1. A student removes the gumballs and labels from the bag.
2. He places a label on each gumball machine.
3. He chooses a gumball, names the place value of the underlined digit, and matches it to the correct gumball machine.
4. He continues in this manner with the remaining gumballs, and then completes the recording sheet on page 92.

Center Options

On a separate sheet of paper, have the student write each answer in expanded notation.

Program the open cards with additional numbers and underlined digits.

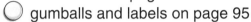

Gumballs Galore

Color the circle to match the backs of your center labels. ◯

Label the gumball machines to match your center labels.
Write each number on the correct gumball machine.

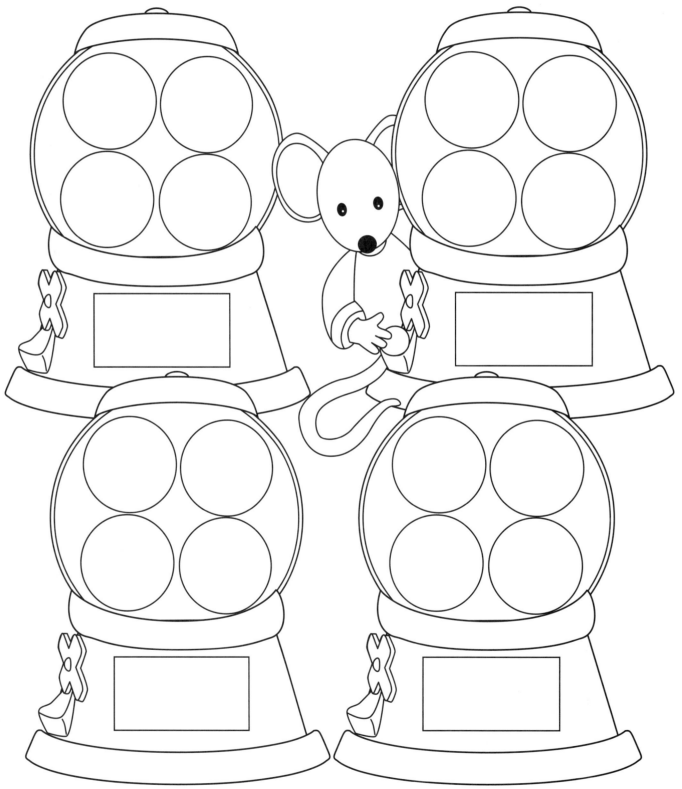

©The Education Center, Inc. • *Centered on Success* • TEC60821 • Key p. 165

92 **Note to the teacher:** Use with the directions on page 91.

Gumballs Galore

1. Place a label on each gumball machine.
2. For each gumball, name the place value of the underlined digit and match it to the correct gumball machine.
3. Complete page 92.

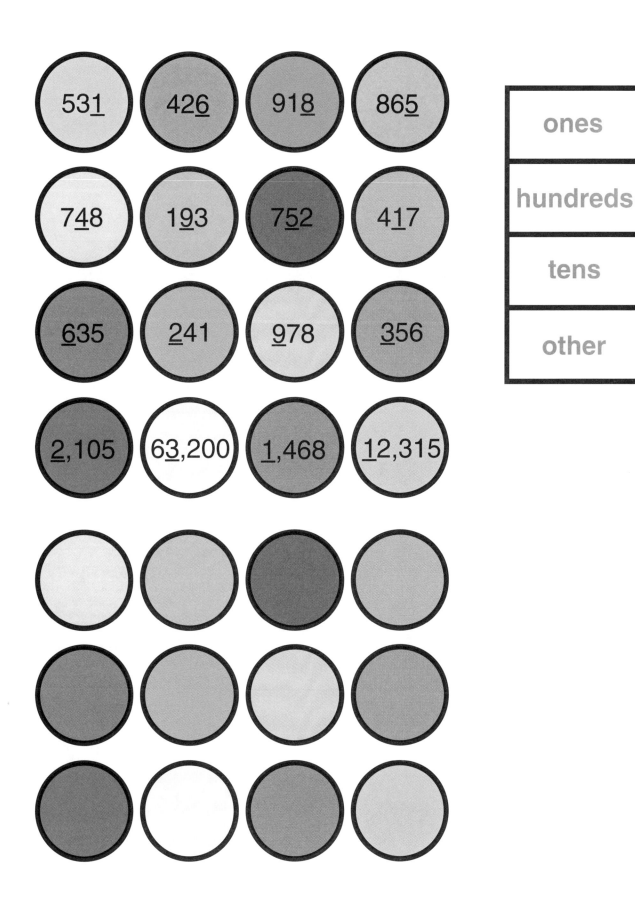

531<u>1</u>	42<u>6</u>	91<u>8</u>	86<u>5</u>
7<u>4</u>8	1<u>9</u>3	75<u>2</u>	4<u>1</u>7
<u>6</u>35	<u>2</u>41	<u>9</u>78	<u>3</u>56
<u>2</u>,105	63,<u>2</u>00	<u>1</u>,468	<u>1</u>2,315

ones
hundreds
tens
other

6,27<u>3</u>   4,51<u>2</u>   1,89<u>5</u>   2,74<u>6</u>

1,4<u>2</u>5   2,3<u>6</u>1   3,5<u>3</u>8   8,0<u>4</u>1

5,<u>2</u>31   6,<u>4</u>73   9,<u>5</u>62   7,<u>3</u>20

<u>1</u>,328   <u>4</u>,156   <u>7</u>,540   <u>3</u>,672

ones
hundreds
tens
thousands

Off to the Zoo!

 Adding basic facts to 10

 Adding basic facts to 18

Materials:
a supply of the recording sheet on page 100
center mat on page 101
 number strips on page 103
number strips on page 105

Preparing the centers:
1. Laminate the center mat and strips.
2. Cut out the strips.
3. Cut slits in the center mat where indicated.
4. Place the strips, center mat, and copies of the recording sheet at a center.

Using the centers:
1. A student inserts the strips into the slits in the center mat.
2. She slides the left strip to show problem A.
3. She slides the right strip to show the answer to problem A.
4. She writes the problem and its answer next to its corresponding letter on the recording sheet on page 100.
5. She continues in this same manner with the remaining problems.

Center Option
On the back of her recording sheet, have each student use the basic facts to write word problems about the animals on the bus.

Name _____

100

Off to the Zoo!

Color the circle to match the backs of your center strips. ◯

Copy problem A and its answer on the lines.
Continue in this same manner with the remaining problems.

A. ____ + ____ = ____

B. ____ + ____ = ____

C. ____ + ____ = ____

D. ____ + ____ = ____

E. ____ + ____ = ____

F. ____ + ____ = ____

G. ____ + ____ = ____

H. ____ + ____ = ____

I. ____ + ____ = ____

J. ____ + ____ = ____

K. ____ + ____ = ____

L. ____ + ____ = ____

Note to the teacher: Use with the directions on page 99.

Off to the Zoo!

1. Insert the strips into the slits.
2. Slide the left strip to show problem A.
3. Slide the right strip to show the answer to problem A.
4. Complete page 100.

ZOO
5 miles

L.   7 + 2 =

K.   1 + 9 =

J.   4 + 4 =

I.   3 + 6 =

H.   5 + 4 =

G.   1 + 4 =

F.   5 + 5 =

E.   10 + 0 =

D.   2 + 2 =

C.   2 + 5 =

B.   4 + 2 =

A.   8 + 0 =

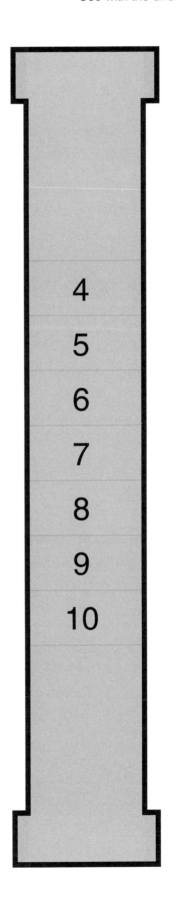

4

5

6

7

8

9

10

L.　6 + 9 =

K.　6 + 7 =

J.　7 + 9 =

I.　4 + 7 =

H.　6 + 6 =

G.　8 + 9 =

F.　6 + 8 =

E.　8 + 7 =

D.　9 + 9 =

C.　8 + 5 =

B.　5 + 9 =

A.　8 + 8 =

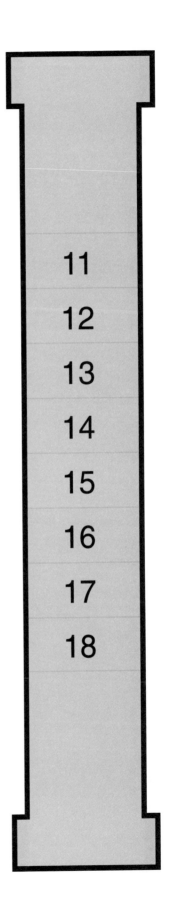

11

12

13

14

15

16

17

18

Wiggle Round the Garden

 Subtracting from 8, 9, and 10

 Subtracting from 11, 13, and 18

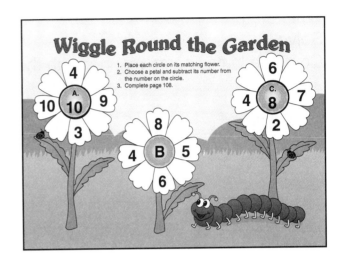

Materials:
supply of the recording sheet on page 108
center mat on page 109
circles and flower manipulatives (optional) on page 111
circles and flower manipulatives (optional) on page 113
2 resealable plastic bags

Preparing the centers:
1. Laminate the center mat, circles, and optional flower manipulatives if desired.
2. Cut out the circles and manipulatives. Put each set into a separate bag.
3. Place the bags, center mat, and copies of the recording sheet at a center.

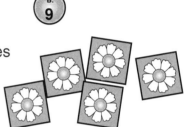

Using the centers:
1. A student removes the circles and manipulatives from the bag.
2. He places each circle in the center of its matching flower.
3. He chooses a petal and subtracts its number from the number on the circle, using the flower manipulatives if needed.
4. He writes the problem and its answer on the corresponding section of the recording sheet on page 108.
5. He continues in this same manner with the remaining petals and flowers.

Center Option
 Store the center materials in a gardening bag or flowerpot.

107

Name_____ *Subtracting*

Wiggle Round the Garden

Color the circle to match the backs of your center circles. ◯

Write the problem from the mat.
Solve.
Continue in this same manner with the remaining petals and flowers.

_____ − _____   _____ − _____   _____ − _____   _____ − _____

_____ − _____   _____ − _____   _____ − _____   _____ − _____

_____ − _____   _____ − _____   _____ − _____   _____ − _____

©The Education Center, Inc. • *Centered on Success* • TEC60821 • Key p. 165

108   **Note to the teacher:** Use with the directions on page 107.

Wiggle Round the Garden

1. Place each circle on its matching flower.
2. Choose a petal and subtract its number from the number on the circle.
3. Complete page 108.

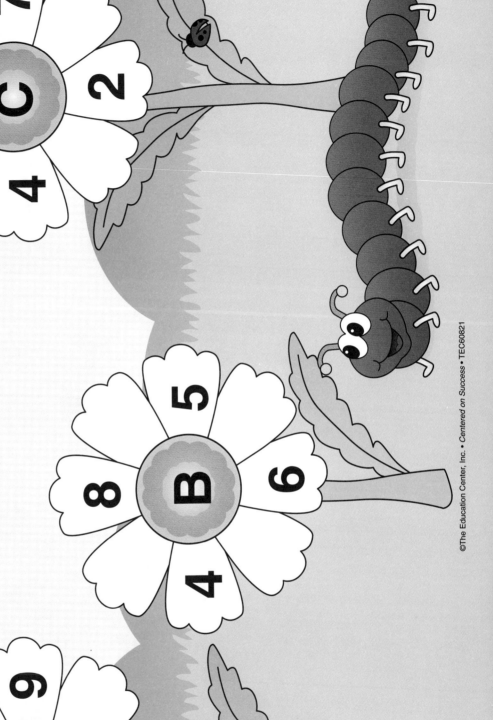

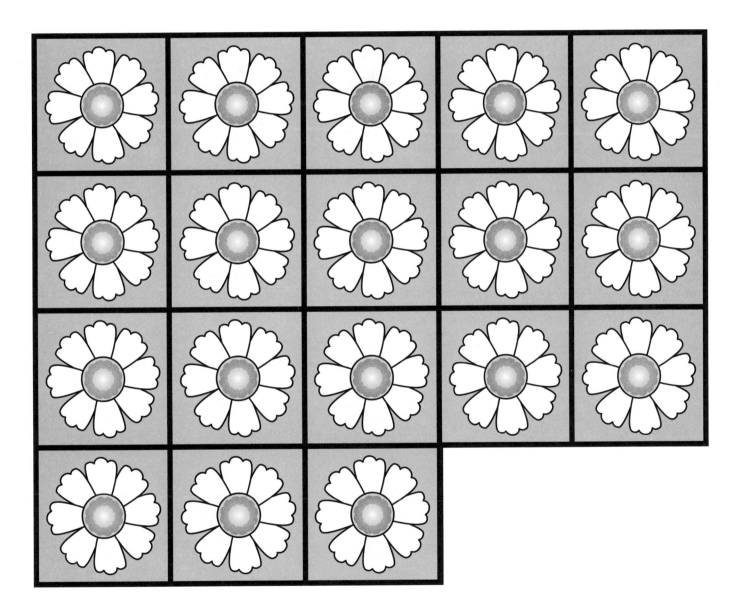

Keep On Tractoring!

 Adding two-digit numbers without regrouping

 Adding two-digit numbers with regrouping

Materials:
supply of the recording sheet on page 116
center mat on page 117
number wheels on page 119
number wheels on page 121
2 brads
2 resealable plastic bags

Preparing the centers:
1. Laminate the center mat and number wheels.
2. Cut out the windows in the center mat and the number wheels.
3. Poke a small hole through the black dot on each number wheel and through each wheel on the center mat.
4. Put each set of number wheels in a separate bag.
5. Place the bags, center mat, brads, and copies of the recording sheet at a center.

Using the centers:
1. A student uses a brad to attach each wheel to the back of the center mat.
2. She turns each wheel to show the number for problem A.
3. She uses the numbers to write an addition problem and solves it on the recording sheet on page 116 beside its corresponding letter.
4. She continues in this same manner with the remaining problems.

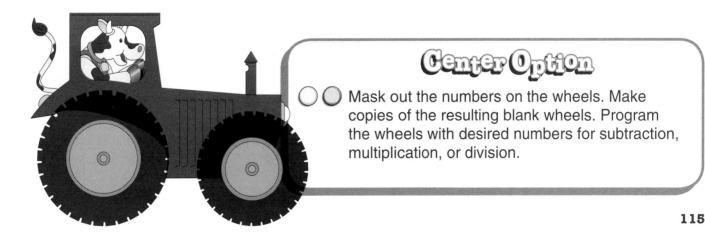

Center Option
Mask out the numbers on the wheels. Make copies of the resulting blank wheels. Program the wheels with desired numbers for subtraction, multiplication, or division.

Name _____

Keep On Tractoring!

Color the circle to match the backs of your center wheels. ◯

Use the numbers shown in the two windows to write an addition problem on a tractor.

Solve.

Continue in this same manner with the remaining numbers.

A.

B.

C.

D.

E.

F.

G.

H.

I.

Note to the teacher: Use with the directions on page 115.

Keep On Tractoring!

1. Attach each wheel to the back of this mat with a brad.
2. Turn each wheel to show the number for problem A.
3. Complete page 116.

Right Wheel

Cut out.

Left Wheel

Cut out.

117

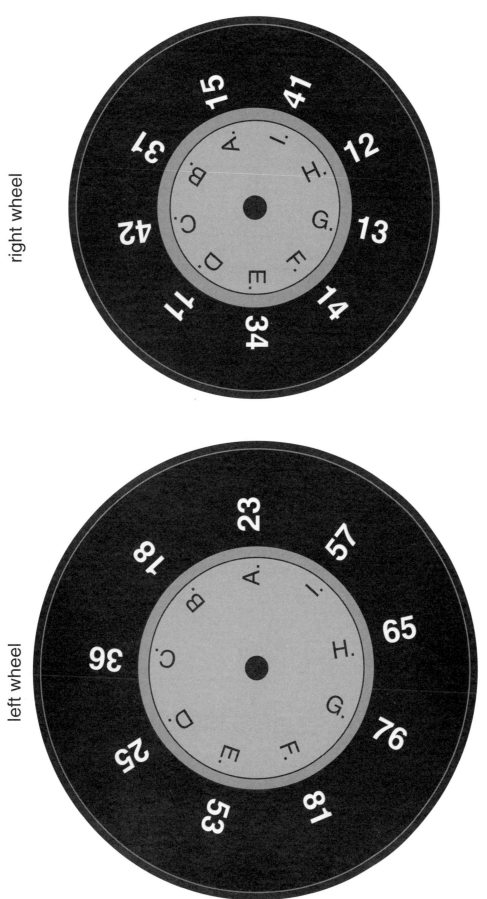

right wheel

left wheel

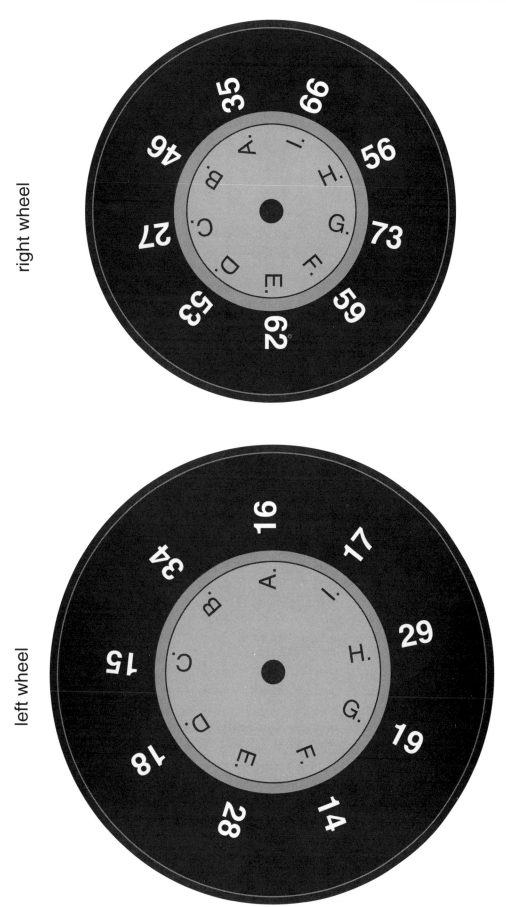

right wheel

left wheel

Game Time!

 Subtracting two-digit numbers without regrouping

 Subtracting two-digit numbers with regrouping

Materials:
supply of the recording sheet on page 124
center mat on page 125
soccer balls on page 127
soccer balls on page 129
2 resealable plastic bags

Preparing the centers:
1. Laminate the center mat and soccer balls if desired.
2. Cut out the balls and put each programmed set into a separate bag.
3. Place the bags, center mat, and copies of the recording sheet at a center.

Using the centers:
1. A student removes the soccer balls from the bag.
2. He chooses a ball, writes the problem on his recording sheet, and solves it.
3. He indicates on his paper whether the answer on the ball is correct.
4. If the answer is correct, he places the ball in the net on the center mat.
5. If the answer is incorrect, he places the ball outside the net.
6. He continues in this same manner with the remaining balls.
7. He adds the number of balls in the net and writes the total number of goals at the bottom of his recording sheet on page 124.

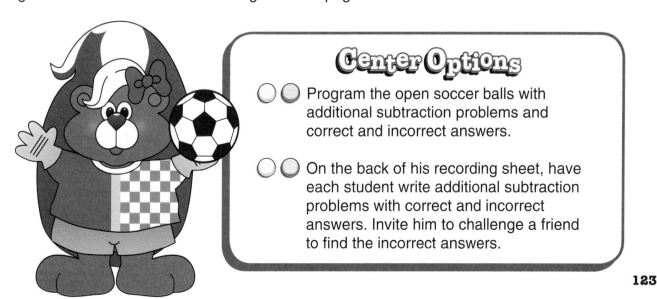

Center Options

Program the open soccer balls with additional subtraction problems and correct and incorrect answers.

On the back of his recording sheet, have each student write additional subtraction problems with correct and incorrect answers. Invite him to challenge a friend to find the incorrect answers.

Game Time!

Color the circle to match the backs of your center soccer balls. ⃝

Write and solve the problem in the first box and answer the question.

If the given answer is correct, place the ball in the net on the center mat.

If the answer is incorrect, place the ball outside the net.

Continue in this same manner with the remaining balls.

Is the answer on the ball correct? _____	Is the answer on the ball correct? ____
Is the answer on the ball correct? _____	Is the answer on the ball correct? ____
Is the answer on the ball correct? _____	Is the answer on the ball correct? ____
Is the answer on the ball correct? _____	Is the answer on the ball correct? ____

How many goals did you score?

Game Time!

1. Choose a soccer ball.
2. Complete page 124.

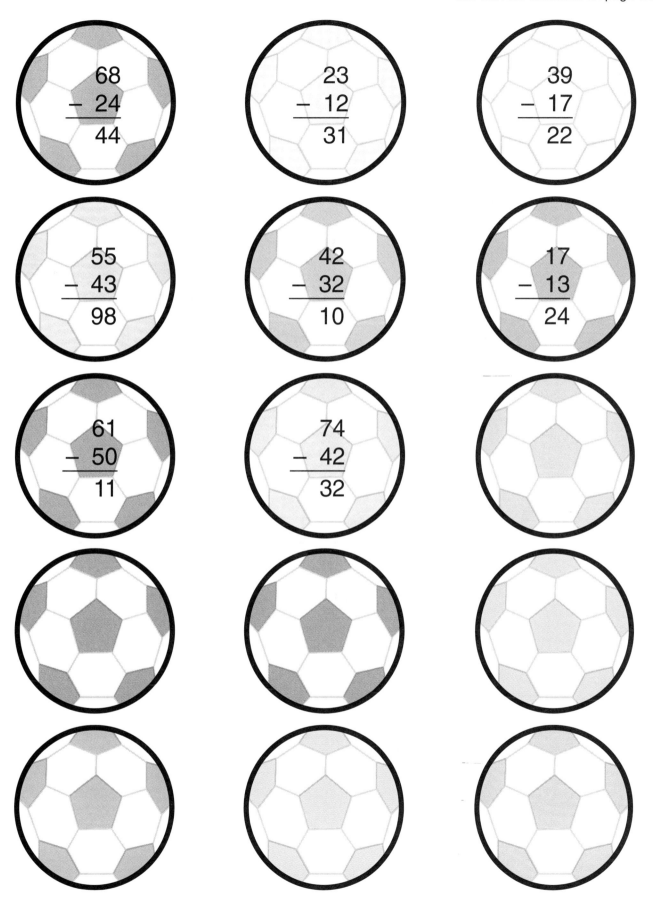

$$\begin{array}{r} 68 \\ -\ 24 \\ \hline 44 \end{array}$$

$$\begin{array}{r} 23 \\ -\ 12 \\ \hline 31 \end{array}$$

$$\begin{array}{r} 39 \\ -\ 17 \\ \hline 22 \end{array}$$

$$\begin{array}{r} 55 \\ -\ 43 \\ \hline 98 \end{array}$$

$$\begin{array}{r} 42 \\ -\ 32 \\ \hline 10 \end{array}$$

$$\begin{array}{r} 17 \\ -\ 13 \\ \hline 24 \end{array}$$

$$\begin{array}{r} 61 \\ -\ 50 \\ \hline 11 \end{array}$$

$$\begin{array}{r} 74 \\ -\ 42 \\ \hline 32 \end{array}$$

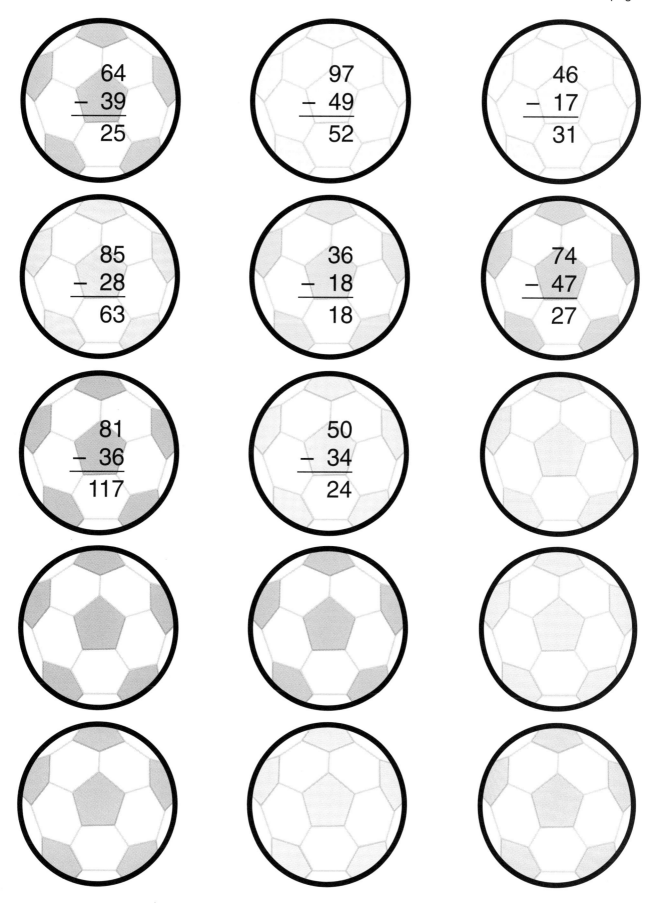

64
− 39
25

97
− 49
52

46
− 17
31

85
− 28
63

36
− 18
18

74
− 47
27

81
− 36
117

50
− 34
24

The Honey Hunt

 Multiplying by 2 and 5

 Multiplying by 3 and 4

Materials:

supply of the recording sheet on page 132
center mat on page 133
○ honey pot and bee cards on page 135
○ honey pot and bee cards on page 137
2 resealable plastic bags

Preparing the centers:

1. Laminate the center mat and cards if desired.
2. Cut out the cards and put each set into a separate bag.
3. Place the bags, center mat, and copies of the recording sheet at a center.

Using the centers:

1. A student removes the cards from the bag.
2. She chooses honey pot card A and places it on the center mat where indicated.
3. She finds the bee card with the matching math sentences and places it on the center mat.
4. She copies the math sentences from the bee card onto page 132 and writes the answers.
5. She removes the cards from the center mat and continues in this same manner with the remaining cards.

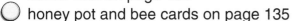

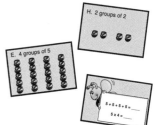

Center Option

○ ○ On the back of her recording sheet, have each student draw groups of honey pots for different multiplication facts. Then have her challenge a classmate to write math sentences and answers to match.

The Honey Hunt

Color the circle to match the backs of your bee cards. ◯

Copy the math sentences from the bee card.
Write the answers.
Continue in this same manner with the remaining cards.

A. _____ = _____

_____ x _____ = _____

B. _____ = _____

_____ x _____ = _____

C. _____ = _____   F. _____ = _____

_____ x _____ = _____   _____ x _____ = _____

D. _____ = _____   G. _____ = _____

_____ x _____ = _____   _____ x _____ = _____

E. _____ = _____   H. _____ = _____

_____ x _____ = _____   _____ x _____ = _____

©The Education Center, Inc. • *Centered on Success* • TEC60821 • Key p. 166

132 **Note to the teacher:** Use with the directions on page 131.

The Honey Hunt

1. Place honey pot card A in the box below.
2. Find the bee card with the matching math sentences.
3. Complete page 132.

Place honey pot card here.

Honey Pot and Bee Cards

Use with the directions on page 131.

A. 4 groups of 2

B. 5 groups of 2

C. 3 groups of 5

D. 6 groups of 2

E. 4 groups of 5

F. 3 groups of 2

G. 5 groups of 5

H. 2 groups of 2

2 + 2 + 2 + 2 = ____

2 x 4 = ____

2 + 2 + 2 + 2 + 2 = ____

2 x 5 = ____

5 + 5 + 5 = ____

5 x 3 = ____

2 + 2 + 2 + 2 + 2 + 2 = ____

2 x 6 = ____

5 + 5 + 5 + 5 = ____

5 x 4 = ____

2 + 2 + 2 = ____

2 x 3 = ____

5 + 5 + 5 + 5 + 5 = ____

5 x 5 = ____

2 + 2 = ____

2 x 2 = ____

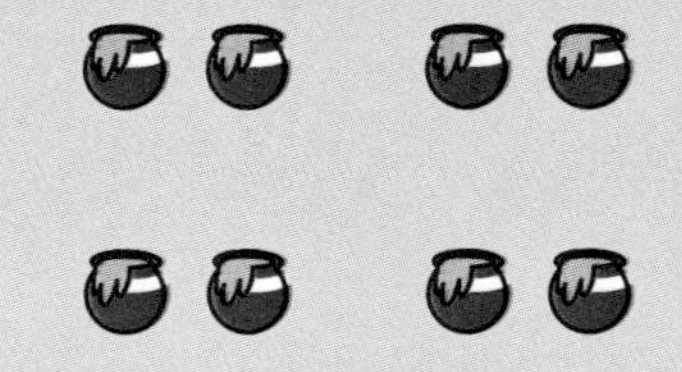

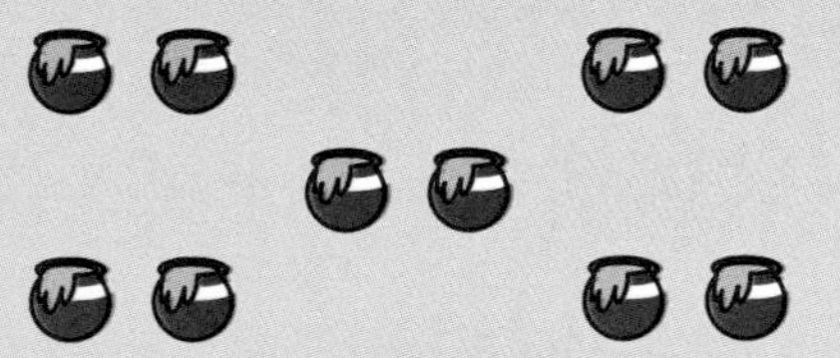

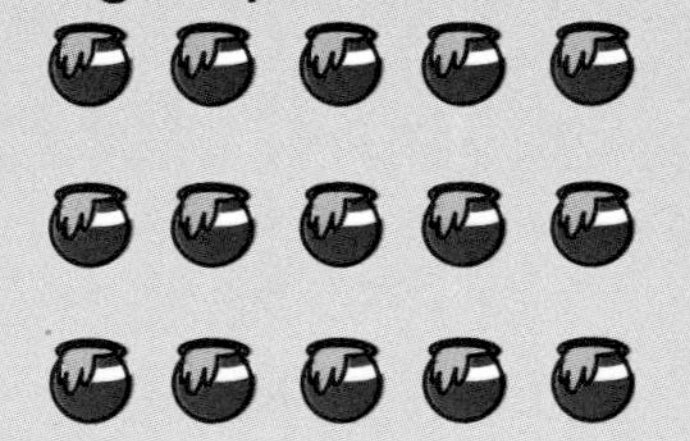

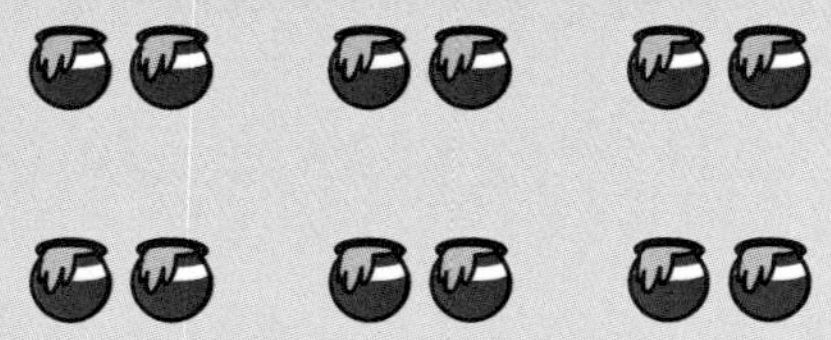

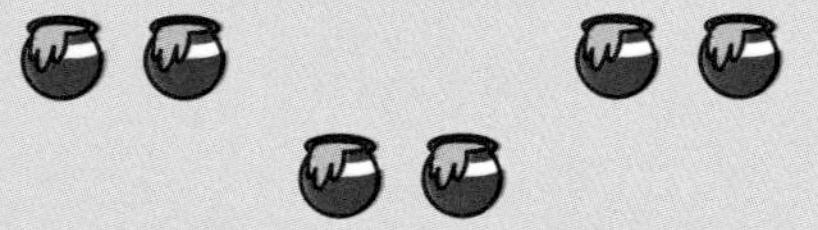

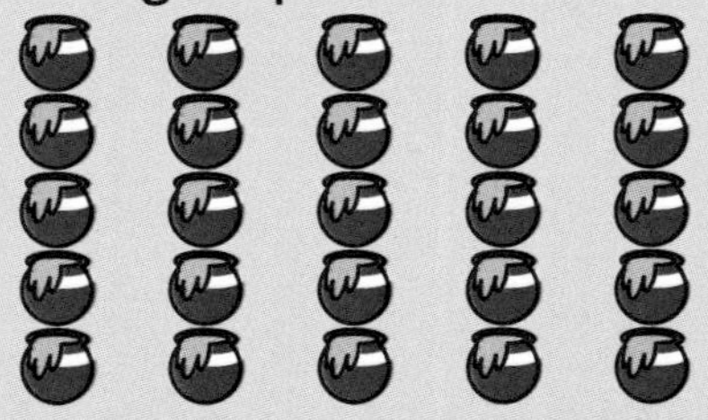

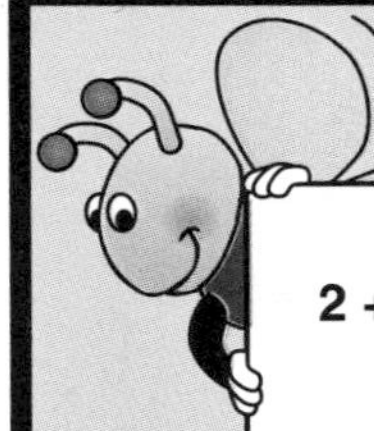

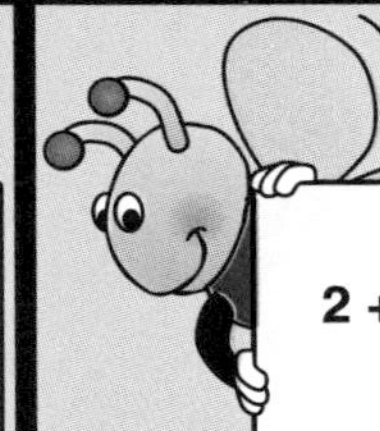

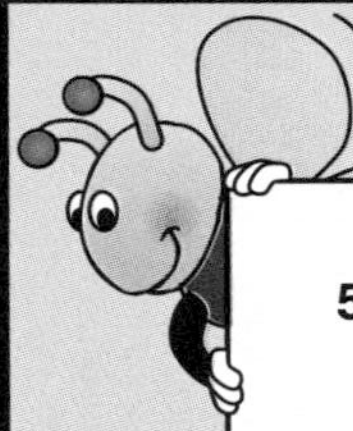

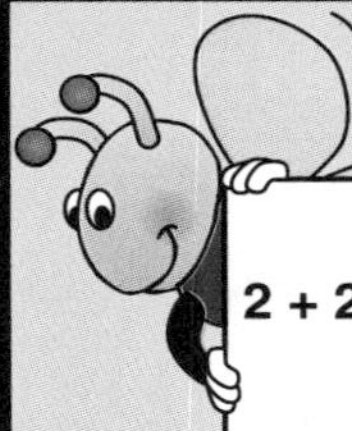

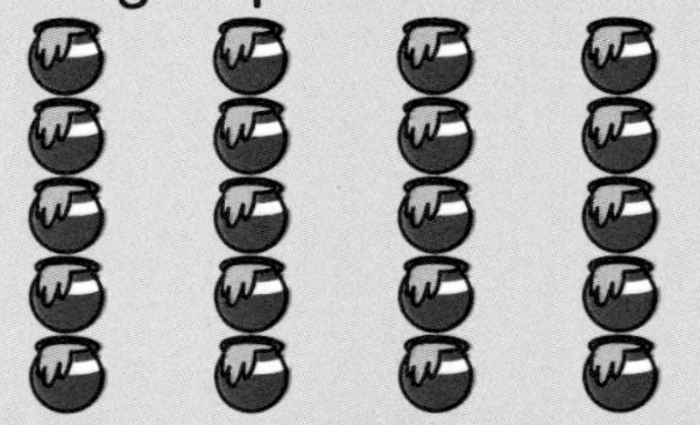

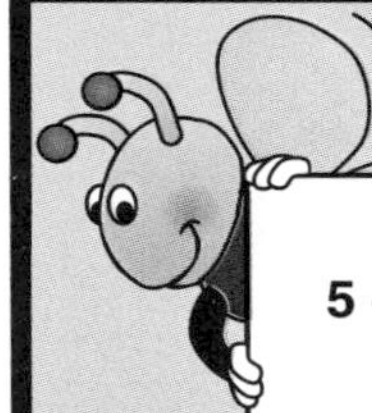

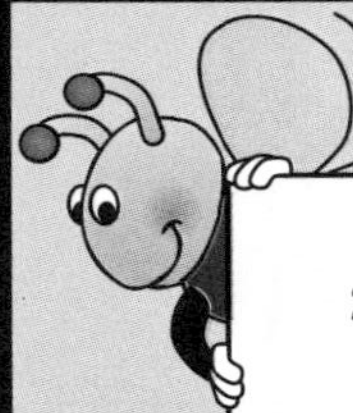

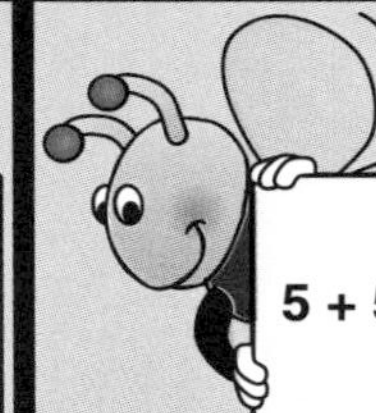

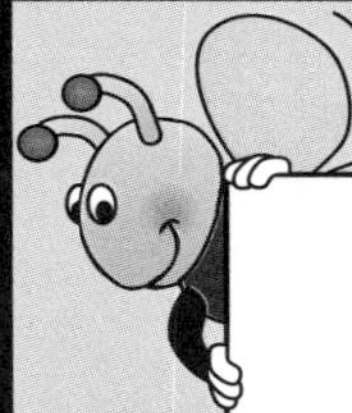

D. 6 groups of 3	C. 4 groups of 3	B. 5 groups of 3	A. 4 groups of 4
H. 2 groups of 3	G. 3 groups of 3	F. 2 groups of 4	E. 3 groups of 4

$3 + 3 + 3 + 3 + 3 + 3 =$ ___
$3 \times 6 =$ ___

$3 + 3 + 3 + 3 =$ ___
$3 \times 4 =$ ___

$3 + 3 + 3 + 3 + 3 =$ ___
$3 \times 5 =$ ___

$4 + 4 + 4 + 4 =$ ___
$4 \times 4 =$ ___

$3 + 3 =$ ___
$3 \times 2 =$ ___

$3 + 3 + 3 =$ ___
$3 \times 3 =$ ___

$4 + 4 =$ ___
$4 \times 2 =$ ___

$3 + 3 + 3 + 3 =$ ___
$4 \times 3 =$ ___

Money in the Bank

 Identifying the value of mixed coins to 75¢

 Identifying the value of mixed coins to $1.00

Materials:
- supply of the recording sheet on page 140
- center mat on page 141
- coins and label on page 143
- coins and label on page 145
- 2 resealable plastic bags
- paper clip
- sharpened pencil

Preparing the centers:
1. Laminate the center mat, coins, and labels.
2. Cut out the coins and labels and put each set into a separate bag.
3. Place the bags, center mat, paper clip, sharpened pencil, and copies of the recording sheet at a center.

Using the centers:
1. A student removes the coins and label from the bag.
2. She lays the label on the center mat where indicated.
3. She uses the pencil and paper clip to make a spinner as shown.
4. She spins the paper clip and places the matching coin on the safe.
5. She continues spinning the number of times indicated on the label.
6. She writes how many of each coin she has on the recording sheet on page 140, and then writes the total cash value of the coins.
7. She removes the coins from the safe and continues in this same manner until the recording sheet is complete.

Center Option

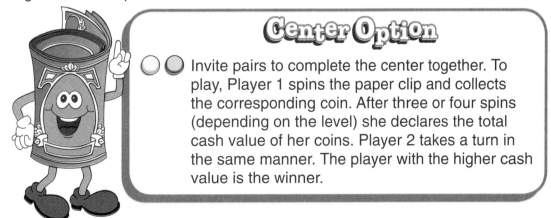

Invite pairs to complete the center together. To play, Player 1 spins the paper clip and collects the corresponding coin. After three or four spins (depending on the level) she declares the total cash value of her coins. Player 2 takes a turn in the same manner. The player with the higher cash value is the winner.

Name _____

140

Money in the Bank

Color the circle to match the backs of your coins. ◯

Write how many of each coin.
Write the total cash value of all the coins on the last line.
Take the coins from the safe.
Continue in this same manner to finish this page.

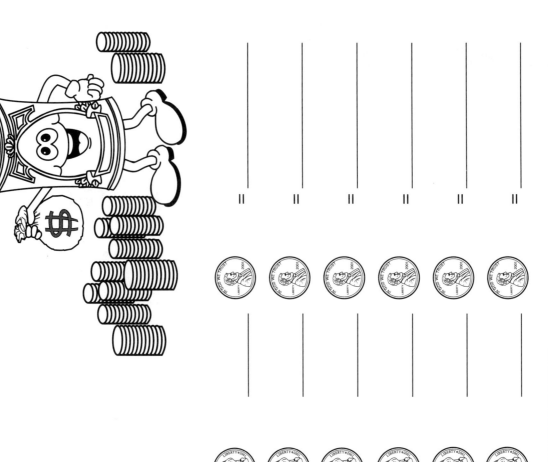

Note to the teacher: Use with the directions on page 139.

Money in the Bank

Place label here.

1. Place the label on the center mat.
2. Use the pencil and paper clip to make a spinner as shown.
3. Spin the paper clip and place the matching coin on the safe.
4. Repeat by spinning the number of times shown on the label.
5. Complete page 140.

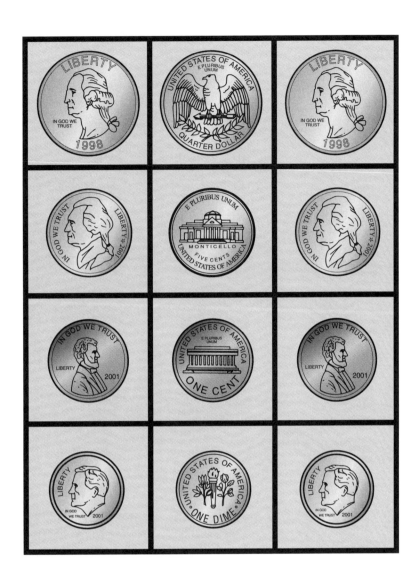

Spin the paper clip 3 times.

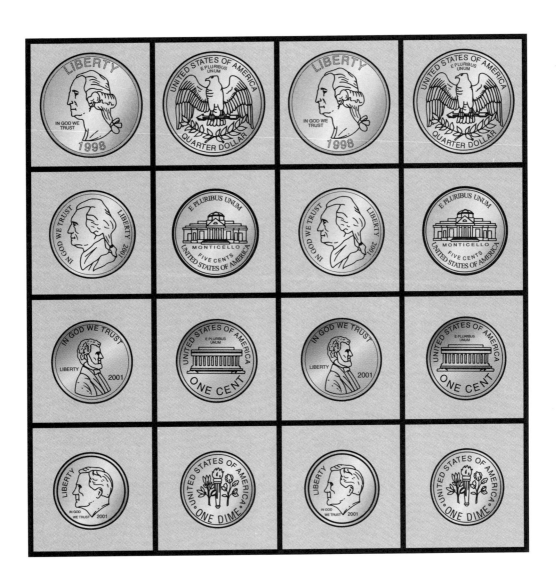

Spin the paper clip 4 times.

Mouse Time

 Telling time: hour, half hour

 Telling time: half hour, quarter hour

Materials:

supply of the recording sheet on page 148
center mat on page 149
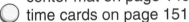 time cards on page 151
time cards on page 153
2 resealable plastic bags
clock hands on page 151
brad

Preparing the centers:

1. Laminate the center mat, clock hands, and time cards if desired.
2. Cut the cards apart and put each programmed set into a separate bag.
3. Cut out the clock hands. Poke the brad through the minute hand, the hour hand, and the clock face on the center mat (in that order); then fasten the brad.
4. Place the bags, center mat, and copies of the recording sheet at a center.

Using the centers:

1. A student removes the time cards from the bag and stacks them in order with card A on top.
2. She selects card A, reads the time, and lays it on the center mat where indicated.
3. She moves the clock hands to show the time.
4. She draws the clock hands on the recording sheet on page 148 to match.
5. She writes the time below the clock.
6. She continues in this same manner with the remaining cards.

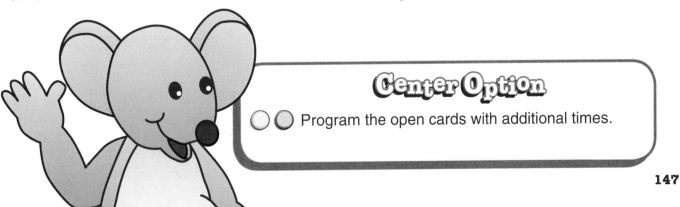

Center Option

Program the open cards with additional times.

Mouse Time

Color the circle to match the backs of your center cards. ◯

Draw clock hands to show the time on card A.
Write the time below clock A.
Continue in this same manner with the remaining cards.

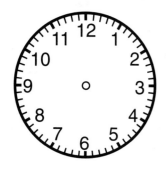
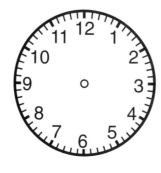
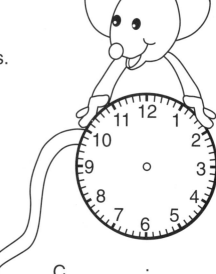

A. _____ : _____   B. _____ : _____   C. _____ : _____

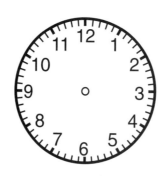
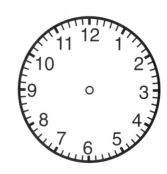

D. _____ : _____   E. _____ : _____   F. _____ : _____

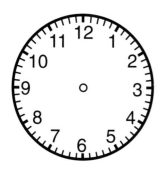
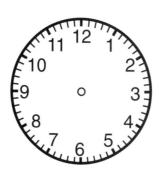
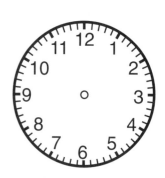

G. _____ : _____   H. _____ : _____   I. _____ : _____

Mouse Time

Place card here.

12
1
2
3
4
5
6
7
8
9
10
11

1. Choose card A and read it.
2. Lay the card on the center mat.
3. Use the clock hands to show the time.
4. Complete page 148.

A. 6:00	B. 5:30	C. 12:00
D. 7:30	E. 10:30	F. 2:00
G. 3:30	H. 4:30	I. 8:30
A. :	B. :	C. :
D. :	E. :	F. :
G. :	H. :	I. :

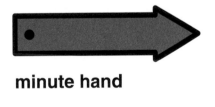

minute hand

hour hand

A. 1:30	B. 9:45	C. 7:45
D. 6:15	E. 10:45	F. 12:30
G. 11:15	H. 8:45	I. 2:15
A. :	B. :	C. :
D. :	E. :	F. :
G. :	H. :	I. :

Treasure Island

 Measuring length to the nearest inch

 Measuring length to the nearest centimeter

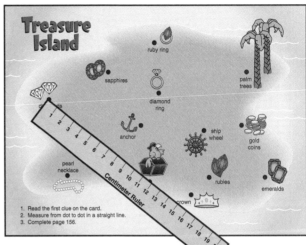

Materials:

supply of the recording sheet on page 156
center mat on page 157
clue card and ruler on page 159
clue card and ruler on page 161

Preparing the centers:

1. Laminate the center mat, clue cards, and rulers if desired.
2. Cut out the cards and rulers.
3. Place the cards, rulers, center mat, and copies of the recording sheet at a center.

Using the centers:

1. A student reads the first clue on the card.
2. He measures the distance on the center mat from dot to dot in a straight line.
3. He writes the measurement on page 156 beside the corresponding number.
4. He continues in this same manner with the remaining clues.
5. He reads the clue for the secret treasure and then writes his answer at the bottom of his recording sheet on page 156.

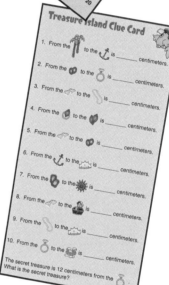

Center Option

Have each student measure the distances between two new pairs of items. Then have him list the items and their distances on the back of his paper.

Name

Treasure Island

Color the circle to match the back of your ruler. ◯

Write the length on its line below.
Continue in this same manner with the remaining clues.

Ahoy, matey!

1. _____

2. _____

3. _____

4. _____

5. _____

6. _____

7. _____

8. _____

9. _____

10. _____

What is the secret treasure? _____

Note to the teacher: Use with the directions on page 155.

Treasure Island

palm trees

gold coins

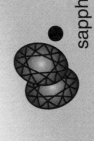
emeralds

ship wheel

rubies

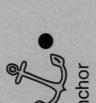

crown

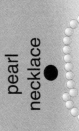

ruby ring

diamond ring

treasure chest

anchor

sapphires

pearl necklace

diamonds

1. Read the first clue on the card.
2. Measure from dot to dot in a straight line.
3. Complete page 156.

©The Education Center, Inc. • *Centered on Success* • TEC60821

157

Treasure Island Clue Card

1. From the 💎 to the 💍 is _____ inches.

2. From the 💍 to the ☸ is _____ inches.

3. From the 🪙 to the 👑 is _____ inches.

4. From the 💠 to the 💜 is _____ inches.

5. From the 🍃 to the 💎 is _____ inches.

6. From the 💜 to the 💍 is _____ inches.

7. From the 💎 to the 🪙 is _____ inches.

8. From the 📿 to the 🦜 is _____ inches.

9. From the 💜 to the 🌴 is _____ inches.

10. From the 🦜 to the ⚓ is _____ inches.

The secret treasure is 2 inches from the  .
What is the secret treasure?

8
7
6
5
4
3
2
1

Inches Ruler

Treasure Island Clue Card

1. From the to the is _____ centimeters.

2. From the to the is _____ centimeters.

3. From the to the is _____ centimeters.

4. From the to the is _____ centimeters.

5. From the to the is _____ centimeters.

6. From the to the is _____ centimeters.

7. From the to the is _____ centimeters.

8. From the to the is _____ centimeters.

9. From the to the is _____ centimeters.

10. From the to the is _____ centimeters.

The secret treasure is 12 centimeters from the .
What is the secret treasure?

Centimeter Ruler

20 19 18 17 16 15 14 13 12 11 10 9 8 7 6 5 4 3 2 1

Answer Keys

Page 4 (Y)

angry
S = mad, A = glad
chilly
S = cold, A = warm
late
S = tardy, A = early
pal
S = friend, A = enemy
neat
S = tidy, A = messy
start
S = begin, A = end
soggy
S = wet, A = dry
big
S = large, A = small
throw
S = toss, A = catch
skinny
S = thin, A = fat
shout
S = yell, A = whisper
above
S = over, A = below

Page 4 (B)

kind
S = nice, A = mean
laugh
S = giggle, A = cry
shut
S = close, A = open
begin
S = start, A = end
correct
S = right, A = wrong
alike
S = same, A = different
boring
S = dull, A = exciting
quick
S = fast, A = slow
grin
S = smile, A = frown
easy
S = simple, A = difficult
sad
S = unhappy, A = happy
buy
S = purchase, A = sell

Page 12 (Y)

back
snack
jack
shack
black
smack
kick
chick
thick
brick
wick
nick

Page 12 (B)

light
might
night
flight
right
slight
joke
poke
stroke
choke
woke
smoke

Page 20 (Y)

Short *a:*
flag
ant

Short *e:*
net
desk

Short *i:*
ring
six

Short *o:*
mop
sock

Short *u:*
drum
duck

Page 20 (B)

Short *a:*
bat
hammer

Long *e:*
cheese
key

Long *i:*
tire
spider

Short *o:*
clock
box

Long *u:*
mule
bugle

Page 28 (Y)

snake
sneeze
sniff
snow
snore
trace
treat
tray
trim
travel

Page 28 (B)

thread
thrill
throat
threat
throw
stream
street
string
strand
straw

Page 36 (Y)

chest
chase
chill
cheese
child
check
shell
shape
shut
short
sharp
shine

Page 36 (B)

chicken
chalk
chomp
shark
share
shirt
rich
such
munch
dash
fish
brush

Page 44 (Y)

ar
barn
jar
shark

or
horn
shorts
fork

ir
third
shirt
girl

Page 44 (B)

ar
yarn
star
arm
scarf

or
forty
horse
cord
thorn

ir
skirt
thirty
first
circle

Page 52 (Y)
renew
rebuild
refill
replay
uneven
unfair
unhappy
unlike

Page 52 (B)
disappear
dishonest
disagree
dislike
preview
prepay
precut
preheat

Page 60 (Y)
helpful
thankful
breakable
enjoyable
fearful
comfortable
washable
careful
cheerful
readable
dependable
colorful

Page 60 (B)
goodness
kindness
harmless
darkness
sickness
spotless
homeless
softness
careless
weakness
endless
timeless

Page 68 (Y)
Answers may vary.
Nouns:
hay
egg
chicken
hat
beak
legs

Not Nouns:
next
other
the
silly

Page 68 (B)
Answers may vary.
Nouns:
feathers
tail
nests
chickens
glasses
friend

Verbs:
sat
wiggle
spin
kick

Page 76 (Y)
We go to the library on **M**ondays.
May is National Book Month.
An author is visiting in **N**ovember.
Wow, the book we read on **W**ednesday
   was so exciting!
Oh, my book was due on **F**riday!
Gee, I can't believe it's **J**une already!
Is the library open on **S**undays?
Will we visit the library in **J**anuary?
Is this book due on **T**uesday?

Page 76 (B)
We are reading books about **T**hanksgiving.
The library is on **M**ain Street.
There is a new computer in the library.
Wow, **H**alloween is in three days!
Gosh, **C**alifornia is a big state!
Gee, this is the best book I've ever read!
Will you read me a **C**hristmas story?
Have you ever read about **A**frica?
Can you take me to Oak **A**venue?

Page 84 (Y)

25, 30, 35, 40, 45, 50, 55, 60
Count by 5s

82, 84, 86, 88, 90, 92, 94, 96
Count by 2s

500, 510, 520, 530, 540, 550, 560, 570
Count by 10s

100, 110, 120, 130, 140, 150, 160, 170
Count by 10s

202, 204, 206, 208, 210, 212, 214, 216
Count by 2s

960, 965, 970, 975, 980, 985, 990, 995
Count by 5s

Page 84 (B)

0, 25, 50, 75, 100, 125, 150, 175
Count by 25s

550, 575, 600, 625, 650, 675, 700, 725
Count by 25s

200, 300, 400, 500, 600, 700, 800, 900
Count by 100s

0, 100, 200, 300, 400, 500, 600, 700
Count by 100s

150, 200, 250, 300, 350, 400, 450, 500
Count by 50s

550, 600, 650, 700, 750, 800, 850, 900
Count by 50s

Page 92 (Y)

ones: 53<u>1</u>, 42<u>6</u>, 91<u>8</u>, 86<u>5</u>
tens: 7<u>4</u>8, 1<u>9</u>3, 7<u>5</u>2, 4<u>1</u>7
hundreds: <u>6</u>35, <u>2</u>41, <u>9</u>78, <u>3</u>56
other: <u>2</u>,105; 63,<u>2</u>00; <u>1</u>,468; <u>1</u>2,315

Page 92 (B)

ones: 6,27<u>3</u>; 4,51<u>2</u>; 1,89<u>5</u>; 2,74<u>6</u>
tens: 1,4<u>2</u>5; 2,3<u>6</u>1; 3,5<u>3</u>8; 8,0<u>4</u>1
hundreds: 5,<u>2</u>31; 6,<u>4</u>73; 9,<u>5</u>62; 7,<u>3</u>20
thousands: <u>1</u>,328; <u>4</u>,156; <u>7</u>,540; <u>3</u>,672

Page 100 (Y)

A. 8 + 0 = 8
B. 4 + 2 = 6
C. 2 + 5 = 7
D. 2 + 2 = 4
E. 10 + 0 = 10
F. 5 + 5 = 10
G. 1 + 4 = 5
H. 5 + 4 = 9
I. 3 + 6 = 9
J. 4 + 4 = 8
K. 1 + 9 = 10
L. 7 + 2 = 9

Page 100 (B)

A. 8 + 8 = 16
B. 5 + 9 = 14
C. 8 + 5 = 13
D. 9 + 9 = 18
E. 8 + 7 = 15
F. 6 + 8 = 14
G. 8 + 9 = 17
H. 6 + 6 = 12
I. 4 + 7 = 11
J. 7 + 9 = 16
K. 6 + 7 = 13
L. 6 + 9 = 15

Page 108 (Y)

A.

10	10	10	10
− 10	− 4	− 9	− 3
0	6	1	7

B.

9	9	9	9
− 4	− 8	− 5	− 6
5	1	4	3

C.

8	8	8	8
− 4	− 6	− 7	− 2
4	2	1	6

Page 108 (B)

A.

18	18	18	18
− 10	− 4	− 9	− 3
8	14	9	15

B.

13	13	13	13
− 4	− 8	− 5	− 6
9	5	8	7

C.

11	11	11	11
− 4	− 6	− 7	− 2
7	5	4	9

Page 116 (Y)

A. 23	B. 18	C. 36
+ 15	+ 31	+ 42
38	49	78

D. 25	E. 53	F. 81
+ 11	+ 34	+ 14
36	87	95

G. 76	H. 65	I. 57
+ 13	+ 12	+ 41
89	77	98

Page 116 (B)

A. 16	B. 34	C. 15
+ 35	+ 46	+ 27
51	80	42

D. 18	E. 28	F. 14
+ 53	+ 62	+ 59
71	90	73

G. 19	H. 29	I. 17
+ 73	+ 56	+ 66
92	85	83

Page 124 Ⓨ
68 – 24 = 44, yes
23 – 12 = 11, no
39 – 17 = 22, yes
55 – 43 = 12, no
42 – 32 = 10, yes
17 – 13 = 4, no
61 – 50 = 11, yes
74 – 42 = 32, yes
Goals scored: 5

Page 124 Ⓑ
64 – 39 = 25, yes
97 – 49 = 48, no
46 – 17 = 29, no
85 – 28 = 57, no
36 – 18 = 18, yes
74 – 47 = 27, yes
81 – 36 = 45, no
50 – 34 = 16, no
Goals scored: 3

Page 132 Ⓨ
A. 2 + 2 + 2 + 2 = 8
    2 x 4 = 8

B. 2 + 2 + 2 + 2 + 2 = 10
    2 x 5 = 10

C. 5 + 5 + 5 = 15
    5 x 3 = 15

D. 2 + 2 + 2 + 2 + 2 + 2 = 12
    2 x 6 = 12

E. 5 + 5 + 5 + 5 = 20
    5 x 4 = 20

F. 2 + 2 + 2 = 6
    2 x 3 = 6

G. 5 + 5 + 5 + 5 + 5 = 25
    5 x 5 = 25

H. 2 + 2 = 4
    2 x 2 = 4

Page 132 Ⓑ
A. 4 + 4 + 4 + 4 = 16
    4 x 4 = 16

B. 3 + 3 + 3 + 3 + 3 + 3 + 3 = 21
    7 x 3 = 21

C. 3 + 3 + 3 + 3 = 12
    3 x 4 = 12

D. 3 + 3 + 3 + 3 + 3 + 3 = 18
    3 x 6 = 18

E. 3 + 3 + 3 + 3 = 12
    4 x 3 = 12

F. 4 + 4 = 8
    4 x 2 = 8

G. 3 + 3 + 3 = 9
    3 x 3 = 9

H. 3 + 3 + 3 + 3 + 3 + 3 + 3 + 3 = 24
    3 x 8 = 24

Page 140 Ⓨ
Answers will vary.

Page 140 Ⓑ
Answers will vary.

Page 148 Ⓨ

A. 6:00

B. 5:30

C. 12:00

D. 7:30

E. 10:30

F. 2:00

G. 3:30

H. 4:30

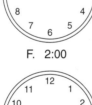
I. 8:30

Page 148 Ⓑ

A. 1:30

B. 9:45

C. 7:45

D. 6:15

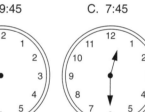
E. 10:45

F. 12:30

G. 11:15

H. 8:45

I. 2:15

Page 156 Ⓨ
1. 4 inches
2. 2 inches
3. 3 inches
4. 2 inches
5. 2 inches
6. 2 inches
7. 7 inches
8. 3 inches
9. 5 inches
10. 2 inches
Secret treasure: gold coins

Page 156 Ⓑ
1. 11 centimeters
2. 5 centimeters
3. 7 centimeters
4. 13 centimeters
5. 6 centimeters
6. 8 centimeters
7. 7 centimeters
8. 12 centimeters
9. 12 centimeters
10. 8 centimeters
Secret treasure: emeralds

Center Management Checklist

Center Title

Student Name

1.	
2.	
3.	
4.	
5.	
6.	
7.	
8.	
9.	
10.	
11.	
12.	
13.	
14.	
15.	
16.	
17.	
18.	
19.	
20.	
21.	
22.	
23.	
24.	
25.	
26.	
27.	
28.	
29.	
30.	

Managing Editor: Kelly Coder
Editor at Large: Diane Badden
Staff Editor: Deborah G. Swider
Concept Developers: Virginia Conrad, Bonnie Mertzlufft
Copy Editors: Tazmen Carlisle, Amy Kirtley-Hill, Kristy Parton, Debbie Shoffner, Cathy Edwards Simrell
Cover Artist: Jennifer Tipton Cappoen
Art Coordinator: Rebecca Saunders
Artists: Jennifer Tipton Cappoen, Pam Crane, Chris Curry, Theresa Lewis Goode, Clevell Harris, Ivy L. Koonce, Clint Moore, Greg D. Rieves, Rebecca Saunders, Barry Slate, Donna K. Teal
The Mailbox® Books.com: Judy P. Wyndham (MANAGER); Jennifer Tipton Cappoen (DESIGNER/ARTIST); Karen White (INTERNET COORDINATOR); Paul Fleetwood, Xiaoyun Wu (SYSTEMS)

President, The Mailbox Book Company™: Joseph C. Bucci
Director of Book Planning and Development: Becky Andrews
Curriculum Director: Karen P. Shelton
Book Development Managers: Cayce Guiliano, Elizabeth H. Lindsay, Thad McLaurin
Editorial Planning: Kimberley Bruck (DIRECTOR); Debra Liverman, Sharon Murphy, Susan Walker (TEAM LEADERS)
Editorial and Freelance Management: Karen A. Brudnak; Sarah Hamblet, Hope Rodgers (EDITORIAL ASSISTANTS)
Editorial Production: Lisa K. Pitts (TRAFFIC MANAGER); Lynette Dickerson (TYPE SYSTEMS); Mark Rainey (TYPESETTER)
Librarian: Dorothy C. McKinney

Manufactured in the United States
10 9 8 7 6 5 4 3